A NEW TREATISE
❧ ON ❧
ACCOMPANIMENT

Publications of the Early Music Institute
Thomas Binkley, general editor

A NEW TREATISE

❧ ON ❧

ACCOMPANIMENT

WITH THE HARPSICHORD, THE ORGAN, AND WITH OTHER INSTRUMENTS

By
Monsieur de Saint Lambert

Translated and edited by
John S. Powell

INDIANA UNIVERSITY PRESS
Bloomington and Indianapolis

The paper used in this publication meets the minimum
requirements of American National Standard for Information Sciences--Permanence of Paper for Printed
Library Materials, ANSI Z39.48-1984.

∞™

Library of Congress Cataloging-in-Publication Data

Saint-Lambert, Michel de
  [Nouveau traité de l'accompagnement du clavecin,
de l'orgue et des autres instruments. English]
  A new treatise on accompaniment with the harpsichord, the organ, and with other instruments / by
Monsieur de Saint Lambert; translated and edited by
John S. Powell.
      p.   cm. -- (Publications of the Early Music In-
stitute)
      Translation of: Nouveau traité de l'accompagne-
ment du clavecin, de l'orgue et des autres instruments.
      Includes bibliographical references.
      ISBN 0-253-34561-8 (alk. paper)
      1. Musical accompaniments--Early works to 1800.
      2. Thorough bass--Early works to 1800
      I. Powell, John S.   II. Title   III. Series.
  MT68.S1513 1991
  786'.147--dc20

                                                90-33591
                                                   CIP
                                                    MN

      1 2 3 4 5   95 94 93 92 91

CONTENTS

Introduction   vii

A New Treatise on Accompaniment

Excerpt of the Privilege   1

Preface   2

Chapter I   Definition of Accompaniment   5

Chapter II   On the Intervals   9

Chapter III   On the Practice of Accompaniment   20

Chapter IV   On Tonality, Mode, & Transposition   47

Chapter V   On the Movement of the Hands   58

Chapter VI   On the Choice of Chords   62

Chapter VII   Rules for Determining the Figures
              when the Thoroughbasses are
              Unfigured   78

Chapter V   On the Licenses that One May Take
              in Accompanying   100

Chapter IX   On Taste in Accompaniment   108

Conclusion   115

Notes   116

INTRODUCTION

The *Nouveau traité de l'accompagnement de clavecin, de l'orgue, et des autres instruments* by Monsieur de Saint Lambert (Paris: Christophe Ballard, 1707) is a significant and influential treatise on keyboard accompaniment that deserves to be better known in its entirety to students of French baroque continuo accompaniment.[1] Saint Lambert's earlier treatise, *Les Principes du clavecin* (Paris: Christophe Ballard, 1702), dealt with the rudiments of musical notation, score reading, and basic keyboard technique; the *Nouveau traité* continues where *Les Principes du clavecin* left off, and thereby completes the training of the beginning harpsichordist.

In the *Nouveau traité* Saint Lambert attempts to logically organize a compendium of rules designed specifically for the keyboard accompanist, rather than for the solo performer. While in *Les Principes du clavecin* we meet Saint Lambert the pedagogue, the *maître du clavecin*, in the *Nouveau traité* we have a better sense of Saint Lambert the performer. After a systematic exposition of the rudiments of 17th-century figured bass theory and notation, Saint Lambert offers his personal insights into the artistic aspects of continuo accompaniment. Here, Saint Lambert evidently draws upon his extensive (but undocumented) experience accompanying both vocalists and instrumentalists. He gives helpful advice to the novice on such problematical topics as realizing unfigured bass and departing from the usual rules for accompanying, and concludes his treatise by attempting to define the elusive component of good taste in accompanying.

Saint Lambert acknowledges in the Preface that his is not the first treatise on accompaniment to appear in France; as F. T. Arnold points out, Saint Lambert includes the adjective *nouveau* in the title to distinguish this treatise from others already in print.[2] Indeed, it would seem that some of Saint Lambert's colleagues discouraged him from publishing the *Nouveau traité* for this very reason. Here in the Preface (p. 2) he defensively states:

The consideration of having been dissuaded by
several people from this endeavor has not at all
stopped me from undertaking it. I am convinced
that, since the minds of men are not all of the
same comprehension & are not of equal disposition
to receive like impressions & ideas about the same
subjects, it would be advantageous that there
might be several Books written on the same sub-
jects--so that those who study them might find in
certain ones that which they often do not come
across in the others.

The earliest thoroughbass treatises in France
dealt initially with theorbo accompaniment, and appeared several decades after similar treatises in
Italy and Germany. The first two published were
Nicolas Fleury's *Méthode pour apprendre facilement à
toucher le théorbe sur la basse-continuë* (Paris,
1660) and Angelo Michele Bartolotti's *Table pour
aprendre à toucher le théorbe sur la basse-continuë*
(Paris, 1669); both of these treatises furnished examples of figured bass realizations in lute tablature. It was not until 1689, with Guillaume-Gabriel
Nivers's *L'Art d'accompagner sur la basse-continue
pour l'orgue et le clavecin* and Jean-Henri d'Anglebert's *Principes de l'accompagnement* (in *Pièces de
clavecin*), that treatises designed specifically for
keyboard accompaniment appeared in France.[3] Denis
Delair's *Traité d'acompagnement pour le théorbe et
le clavessin* (Paris, 1690), and Marc-Antoine Charpentier's brief manuscript, *Abrège des Règles de
l'Accompagnement* [c. 1690; included at the end of
his *Règles de Composition*],[4] soon followed. A decade
later, Jacques Boyvin published his *Traité abrégé
d'accompagnement pour l'orgue et pour le clavessin*
in his *Second livre d'orgue* (Paris, 1700). For
questions that may arise with regard to seventeenth-
century theory, Saint Lambert in the Preface to his
Nouveau traité refers the reader to three contemporary publications: the composition treatises of
Nivers (*Traité de la composition de musique* [Paris,
1667]) and Masson (*Nouveau traité des règles de la
composition de la musique par lequel on apprend à
faire facilement un chant sur des paroles* [Paris,
1694]), and Sebastien de Brossard's *Dictionnaire de*

musique, contenant une explication des termes grecs, latins, italiens, et françois les plus usitez dans la musique (Paris, 1703). Saint Lambert's rules may well derive partly from the treatises of Delair, d'Anglebert, and Boyvin;[5] specific influences, however, are difficult to trace since many of these ideas on thoroughbass realization were common property in the late seventeenth century.

Saint Lambert's *Nouveau traité* stands roughly at the midpoint of a succession of French accompaniment treatises that appeared between 1660 and 1764. His was followed by Jean-Philippe Rameau's *Principes d'Accompagnement* (contained in Book IV of his *Traité de l'harmonie réduite à ses principes naturels,* (Paris, 1722), Denis Delair's revised *Nouveau traité d'accompagnement* (Paris, 1723 [1724]), Michel Corrette's *Le maître de clavecin pour l'accompagnement, methode theorique et pratique* (Paris, 1753), Claude de La Porte's *Traité théorique et pratique de l'accompagnement du clavecin* (Paris, 1754), Charles François Clement's *Essai sur l'accompagnement du clavecin, pour parvenir facilement & en peu de tems à accompagner avec des chiffres ou sans chiffres par les principes les plus clairs & les plus simples de la composition* (Paris, 1758), and Pierre-Joseph Roussier's *Traité des accords et de leur succession, selon le système de la basse-fondamentale* (Paris and Lyon, 1764).

Saint Lambert's theoretical works were well known and widely quoted by eighteenth-century theorists. Upon publication of *Les Principes du clavecin*, Brossard in his *Dictionaire de musique* (Paris, 1703) cited Saint Lambert among the "Auteurs qui ont écrit en françois...que j'ay vus, lus, et examinez moy-même." The Bibliothèque Nationale in Paris possesses six manuscript pages of notes taken by Etienne Loulié from *Les Principes du clavecin*.[6] After the *Nouveau traité* appeared in print, the July 1708 issue of the *Journal de Trévoux* published a review praising both of Saint Lambert's treatises in the highest terms.[7] Rameau indirectly paid homage to Saint Lambert's accompaniment treatise in his monumental *Traité de l'harmonie réduite à ses principes naturels* (Paris, 1722; *Livre quatrième: Principes d'Accompagnement*), where, oddly, Rameau cribbed rel-

atively insignificant passages (without acknowledg-
ment of their source) from the first two chapters of
the *Nouveau traité*.[8]

Saint Lambert's writings were also known to German theorists. Johann David Heinichen's twice refers to the *Nouveau traité* in *Der General-Baß in der
Composition* (Dresden, 1728; pp. 93 and 133), but
this gives little indication of his debt to Saint
Lambert's treatise on accompaniment; George Buelow
points out that much of Heinichen's discussion on
good taste in music comes directly from Saint Lambert's ninth chapter, *De gout de l'accompagnement*.[9]
Saint Lambert's teachings were cited by Johann Mattheson (*Große General-Baß-Schule* [Hamburg, 1731], pp.
12, 51, 127, 351, 413, 425, 450, 455-56, and 463)
and Jacob Adlung (*Anleitung zu der musikalischen
Gelahrheit* [Erfurt, 1758], pp. 212-13, 635, 729-30,
and 789). While Mattheson takes exception with some
of Saint Lambert's opinions, the space he devotes to
quoting and disputing the *Nouveau traité* is testi-
mony of its influence.

Given the extent to which his theoretical works
were known and discussed, it is strange that rela-
tively little information survives on the life and
career of Saint Lambert;[10] indeed, even his first
name and dates remain a mystery. Both French and
German biographical sources have perpetuated misinformation about Saint Lambert and his works. Johann
Gottfried Walther (*Musikalisches Lexikon* [Leipzig,
1732]) correctly attributes *Les Principes du clavecin* and the *Nouveau traité* to "Lambert [de Saint],"
but he also credits Saint Lambert with an instrumental trio along with the court title of "Maître de la
Musique de la Chambre du Roy." Walther evidently
confused Saint Lambert with Michel Lambert (1610-
96)--composer, singer, singing teacher, and father-
in-law of Jean-Baptiste Lully. François-Joseph
Fétis's *Biographie universelle des musiciens* (Paris,
1835-44; VII, 371) corrects Walther's errors, but
retains the first name "Michel" that was mistakenly
given to Saint Lambert by earlier German lexicographers who, like Walther, confused the two musicians.[11] Saint Lambert's name appears on the title
pages of his two treatises simply as "*Monsieur* de

Saint Lambert" (italics mine), and there exists no
evidence proving Michel to be his first name.[12]

Fétis also claims that the *Nouveau traité* predates *Les Principes du clavecin*, and that both treatises appeared earlier. According to Fétis, Saint
Lambert first published the *Nouveau traité* in 1680,
and then he came out with a second edition in 1707;
also, Fétis states that *Les Principes du clavecin*
was published first in 1697 and then later in 1702.[13]
This claim is clearly disproven by the 1702 Preface
to *Les Principes du clavecin*, where Saint Lambert
offers to correct any errors in *Les Principes du
clavecin* "should a second edition be made."[14] In
fact, a second edition was later published by Esti-
enne Roger in Amsterdam, but there is no evidence
that Saint Lambert took any active part in this publication. In the 1707 Preface to the *Nouveau traité*
(p. 2), Saint Lambert remarks that the present treatise was an afterthought to *Les Principes du clavecin*; so there can be little doubt that *Les Principes
du clavecin* predates the *Nouveau traité*, and that
the 1702 and 1707 publications are both first editions.

Saint Lambert's prose style suggests an experienced teacher and practicing accompanist writing
from the vantage point of middle-age: in both treatises he cites works by d'Anglebert, Campra, Cham-
bonnières, Charpentier, Corelli, Lebègue, Lully, and
Nivers published in the late-seventeenth century.
Moreover, in *Les Principes du clavecin* Saint Lambert
remarks on Lully's tempi in *Armide*--first performed
and published in 1686. Saint Lambert's wording in
this passage suggests that he may have attended a
performance of *Armide* under Lully's direction, one
year before the composer's death.[15] If Saint Lambert
had been a young man in 1686 when he might have seen
Lully's *Armide* and middle-aged (as his prose style
suggests) in 1707 when the *Nouveau traité* was published, it seems likely that he was born sometime
during 1650-70.

The *Nouveau traité* aims at helping the beginning
accompanist to play the preferred harmony for a
given situation, without the necessity of reading
all of the parts notated in the score at the same
time. Saint Lambert lists thirty-four figured-bass

signatures, eleven more than in Delair's table of
signatures (*Traité d'accompagnement*, p. 30). Both
authors attempt to help the accompanist classify and
realize a large number of seemingly unrelated figures. In fact, Saint Lambert's method for relating
unfamiliar or uncommon figures to triads built on
other bass notes may derive in part from Delair's
more comprehensive treatment of this subject.

Saint Lambert's directions for substituting different chords for those indicated by the figures reveals a liberal attitude toward playing "correct"
harmony. Moreover, his advice on consecutive perfect intervals is practical rather than academic.
For instance, Saint Lambert permits consecutive
fifths and octaves while accompanying a large ensemble, because here the offensive voice-leading would
be obscured by other parts. Saint Lambert is progressive in the area of notational reform. He advocates such changes as (1) including a full comple-
ment of flats in minor-mode flat keys, (2) reducing
the number of clef signs in use, and (3) accurately
placing continuo figures horizontally relative to
the bass line so as to reflect where changes of
harmony occur.

On other subjects, Saint Lambert proves to be
more conservative. For instance, he omits many of
the augmented intervals from his discussion of the
figures, and forbids the doubling of dissonances in
filled-in accompaniment. Mattheson (*Große General-
Baß-Schule*, "Letztes Prob=Stück der Ober=Claße," 12,
pp. 449-50) found that Saint Lambert labelled as
"rare" certain tonalities that were increasingly being used by composers. Here Mattheson takes exception with F#-minor, and ridicules Saint Lambert's
use of old-fashioned hexachord terminology: "Monsieur St. Lambert calls this tonality *F Ut Fa Dièze
mineur* on p. 29, and he writes under it 'Rare'; *Fis
mol* [F#-minor] is shorter said, and nothing rare to
me." George Buelow identifies in Saint Lambert a
taste for "a decidedly conservative style of composition that seems more suited to music for the
church than for the opera house."[16] Perhaps this is
another biographical clue--which suggests that Saint
Lambert may have served as a church musician.

Saint Lambert was among the first theorists to distinguish between the legato style of organ accompaniment in few parts, and the filled-in style of accompaniment appropriate to the harpsichord. Kenneth Gilbert remarks that Saint Lambert's musical examples in four parts are scholastic and probably do not reflect the actual keyboard practice of the time;[17] although this may well be true with regard to contemporary harpsichord practice, Saint Lambert designed his examples for the organ as well--for which a filled-in style would be unsuitable.

By far the most valuable contributions to the art of accompaniment can be found in the final three chapters of the *Nouveau traité*. Saint Lambert has more to say than his contemporaries on the harmonization of unfigured bass progressions; Chapter Seven concerns accompanying from unfigured and partly-figured basses, for which Saint Lambert codifies bass progressions and assigns appropriate harmonies. In Chapter Eight Saint Lambert allows the accompanist particular liberties--provided that he bears in mind the subservient role of the accompaniment; these include (1) using a single chord to accompany several bass notes, (2) adding or changing notes in the bass, (3) shifting registers in either hand, and (4) permitting consecutive fifths and octaves between parts or between one part and the bass. Saint Lambert's ninth and final chapter examines possible refinements, with the aim of achieving not merely a correct but an artistic accompaniment. In his detailed description of recitative performance he describes techniques used by "tasteful" accompanists--allowing a chord to die away so that the voice sings several notes without accompaniment, discretely repeating single notes from a held chord, and repeating the notes of a chord in random repetition while building to a climax on a single struck chord. In sum, Saint Lambert packs his *Nouveau traité de l'accompagnement* with much practical advice for the beginning accompanist. Notwithstanding certain progressive ideas on notational reform and his liberal attitude toward consecutive fifths and chord-substitutions, Saint Lambert through his harmonic practices reveals himself to be essentially a

conservative musician rooted in the musical style of
the latter part of the seventeenth century.

This edition has been prepared primarily with the
student of early music in mind. To this end, the
translation attempts to strike a balance between
literal translation and readability. English cog-
nates have been used when they correspond in meaning
to the original French; but when another English
word better serves the meaning, the editor substituted it. To simplify the author's complex and
sometimes convoluted syntax, the editor has resorted
to a liberal use of dashes and parentheses; editorial additions within the text are enclosed in
square brackets. References to page numbers of the
original source (repr. Geneva: Minkoff, 1974) have
been placed in the margins. For musical concepts
that may have been in a state of transition at the
time this treatise was written (e.g., *modulation*),
the editor has consulted contemporaneous theoretical
writings--including, of course, Saint Lambert's own
Les Principes du clavecin of 1702. For more general
musical terms that held specific meanings (e.g.,
corde) or numerous meanings (e.g., *ton*) for the seventeenth and eighteenth centuries, the *Encyclopédie*
(1751-65) has served as a useful reference source.

Musical examples are transcribed in the notational style most familiar to modern readers. C-
clefs, used to notate the right-hand accompaniment,
have been replaced by G-clefs; note-shapes are mod-
ernized, and faulty note-alignment has been tacitly
corrected; repeated accidentals within the measure
are suppressed in accordance with modern practice;
and redundant inflections within key-signatures have
been eliminated. In the instance of repeated accidentals whose presence is indicated by the figures
(e.g., Ex. 52 m. 2 has an f# on the downbeat, and
later 6# on bass note A), the repeated accidental
has been retained. For ease in reading Examples 89
and 90, diamond shaped notes have been substituted
for the *guidons* used in the source (see Example 53
for an example where the source *guidons* have been
retained). Three eighteenth-century features of
Saint Lambert's examples have, however, been pre-
served: metric symbols, continuo figures (and their

placement above the bass line), and accidentals contained in the continuo figures (including flats used
to cancel sharps). Corrected accidentals are placed
within square brackets, and parentheses enclose cau-
tionary accidentals. Other editorial corrections to
the examples are cited immediately below the example
using the familiar system of pitch identification
(c' = middle C; c" = the octave above middle C,
etc.). Double barlines have been consistently added
at the end of the examples.

Particular thanks are due to the Henry Kendall
College of Arts and Sciences at the University of
Tulsa for financial assistance and for the use of
computer facilities, to Jay Thompson and to William
Heinrichs for the computer-generated musical examples, to my wife, Helen, for proofreading the various versions of my manuscript, and to Natalie Wrubel
of Indiana University Press for her editorial assistance.

NOTES TO THE INTRODUCTION

1. An extensive discussion of Saint Lambert's
treatise with examples and portions of his text
given in English translation appears in F. T.
Arnold, *The Art of Accompaniment from a Thorough-
Bass* (London: Oxford University Press, 1931), pp.
172-202. Saint Lambert's *Nouveau traité* has twice
been translated: Harold Edward Wills, *Nouveau traité
de l'accompagnement du clavecin de l'orgue et des
autres instruments (1707) by Michel de Saint Lambert: A Translation from the French with Commentary*
(M.A. thesis, The American University, 1978); and
James F. Burchill, *Saint-Lambert's "Nouveau traité
de l'accompagnement": a Translation with Commentary*
(Ph.D. dissertation, The University of Rochester,
1979). The latter is an exceptionally fine and in-
formative study of Saint Lambert's treatise; the in-
ternal inconsistencies that Burchill finds within
the *Nouveau traité* have been cited here in the
notes.
2. Arnold, *The Art of Accompaniment from a Thorough-Bass*, pp. 900-901.

3. Included in his *Motets à voix seule accompag-
nées de la basse continue et quelques autres motets
à deux voix, propres pour les religieuses* (Paris:
l'auteur, 1689); discussed in William Pruitt, "The
Organ Works of G. G. Nivers (1632-1714)," *Recherches
sur la musique française classique*, 14 (1974), pp.
39-42.

4. Published in facsimile and translated in
Lillian M. Ruff, "Marc-Antoine Charpentier's *Règles
de composition*," *The Consort*, 24 (1967), pp. 254-55
and p. 270; but see also Patricia M. Ranum, "Etienne
Loulié (1654-1702): Musicien de Mlle de Guise, péda-
gogue et théoricien," *Recherches sur la musique
française classique*, XXV (1987), pp. 71-72.

5. It is doubtful that Saint Lambert knew of
Charpentier's brief treatise, as it was never published.

6. F-Pn, fonds française, n.a. 6355, fols. 124-
26v. Cited in *Principles of the Harpsichord by Monsieur de Saint Lambert*, trans. and ed. by Rebecca
Harris-Warwick (Oxford University Press, 1984), p.
x.

7. "Mémoires pour l'histoire des Sciences et des
beaux Arts" (*Journal de Trévoux*; juillet 1708).
Facs. ed., Geneva: Slatkine Reprints, 1968, pp.
1257-61. This review, by a self-acknowledged musical amateur, affords little insight into the criti-
cal reception of Saint Lambert's treatises.

8. See *Jean-Philippe Rameau, Treatise on Harmony*,
trans. Philip Gossett (New York: Dover Publications,
1971), pp. xii-xv. These passages are given for
purposes of comparison in the notes to the present
edition.

9. *Thorough-Bass Accompaniment according to
Johann David Heinichen* (University of California
Press, 1966) p. 18.

10. A more detailed examination of the biographical information summarized here is found in *Principles of the Harpsichord by Monsieur de Saint Lambert*, trans. and ed. by Rebecca Harris-Warrick, pp.
viii-ix.

11. See Ernst Ludwig Gerber, *Historisch-Biographisches Lexikon der Tonkünstler* (Leipzig, 1790-
92), p. 777; *idem, Neues Historisch-Biographisches
Lexikon der Tonkünstler* (Lepizig, 1812-14), III,

163; Gustav Schilling, *Encyclopädie der gesammten musikalischen Wißenschaften* (Stuttgart, 1840), IV, 307-08.

12. Yet Saint Lambert's spurious first name still appears on the modern title-page of the reprint of the *Nouveau traité de l'accompagnement* (Genève: Minkoff, 1974), as well as in the *National Union Catalogue*.

13. Rebecca Harris-Warrick (*Principles of the Harpsichord by Monsieur de Saint Lambert*, pp. viii, n. 3) traces this chain of misinformation through the German lexicographers.

14. Fétis's earlier dates for these two treatises were initially accepted by Arnold (*The Art of Accompaniment from a Thorough-Bass*, pp. 172 ff.); but Arnold later decided (pp. 900-01) that the earlier editions were a myth.

15. Evidence that Saint Lambert attended Lully's performance of *Armide* is open to question, and so the relevant passage is given below to enable the reader to construe Saint Lambert's meaning:

> Cette signification peu déterminée des Signes, est un défaut dans l'Art dont les Musiciens ne sont pas garans, & qu'il faut leur pardonner sans difficulté; mais ce dont on pourroit les reprendre avec quelque raison, est que souvent le même Homme marque du même Signe, deux Airs d'un mouvement tout different: comme par exemple, Mr de Lully, qui fait jouer la reprise de l'ouverture d'Armide tres vîte, & l'Air de la page 93. du même Opera tres lentement, quoy que cet Air & la reprise de l'ouverture soient marquez tous deux du Signe de six pour quatre; qu'ils ayent l'un & l'autre six Noires dans la Mesure, & distribuées de la même sorte. Je ne prétens pas pour cela condamner Mr de Lully; Il a pû prendre cette licence, puis que son Art le luy permettoit; mais je voudrois que les Musiciens corrigeassent entre eux cette imperfection dans la Musique qui fait que la théorie est démentie par la pratique. (*Les Principes du clavecin*, p. 25)

16. *Thorough-Bass Accompaniment*, p. 34.

17. Preface to his edition of d'Anglebert's *Pièces de clavecin* (Paris: Heugel, 1975), p. vii.

A NEW TREATISE
ON
ACCOMPANIMENT

By Letters Patent from the King, given at Arras
the eleventh day of the month of May, the Year of
Grace one thousand six hundred and seventy-three,
signed LOUIS; and below, for the King, COLBERT;
sealed by the great Seal with yellow wax: verified &
registered in Parliament, on 15 April 1678. Con-
firmed by countersigned Orders of the Privy Council
of the King on 30 September 1694 & 8 August 1696.
Permission is granted to Christophe Ballard, sole
Printer of Music to the King, to print, to have
printed, to sell & to distribute all types of Music,
both vocal and instrumental, by all authors: all
other persons of whatever rank & station are forbidden to undertake or arrange for the aforesaid print-
ing of Music, or other things of this concern, any-
where throughout the Kingdom, Lands & Domains of his
allegiance, notwithstanding any Letters to the contrary; nor likewise to carve nor to cast any musical
characters [i.e., musical type] without the leave &
permission of the aforesaid Ballard, upon the pen-
alty of confiscation of the aforesaid Characters &
Impressions, & of a fine of six thousand *livres*, in
such a manner as is more fully proclaimed in the
aforesaid Letters: His aforesaid Majesty intends,
with the Extract of this [privilege] placed at the
beginning or at the end of the aforesaid printed
Books, that it be as legally binding as the Original.

This Treatise sells for   2 *livres*
  The *Principles of the Harpsichord* sells for   2 *livres*
    Both Books bound together   5 *livres*

PREFACE

Having previously given the Public a Work entit-
led *Principles of the Harpsichord*[1] in which I discuss
only that which concerns Pieces [i.e., solo harpsichord compositions], I have felt that the title
would not be adequate unless I were to add a *Treatise* on Accompaniment. The consideration of having
been dissuaded by several people from this endeavor
has not at all stopped me from undertaking it. I am
convinced that, since the minds of men are not all
of the same comprehension & are not of equal disposition to receive like impressions & ideas about the
same subjects, it would be advantageous that there
might be several Books written on the same subjects
--so that those who study them might find in certain
ones that which they often do not come across in the
others.[2] Experience teaches us that a new manner of
explaining a Principle often sheds new light on it;
and since the intellects [*genies*] of those who learn
the Sciences and the Arts are sometimes quite different, it is necessary also to have Teachers of
different characters so that each Student might find
one that suits himself. Now, the Methods [i.e., the
instruction manuals] developed to teach a Science or
an Art are like portable Teachers that have the advantage over the others [i.e., the human teachers]
in that they are a much better bargain, & furthermore they may be consulted at any time. One therefore cannot have too many of them, since this offers
each [student] the convenience of choice.

In this Treatise I discuss neither the knowledge
of Notes nor of the Keyboard. I assume that those
who wish to learn Accompaniment have already been
taught these things; but if it so happens that they
have not, they may then turn to the *Principles of
the Harpsichord*--which, provided before this Treatise, serves very naturally as its preparation.[3]

Having now explained the motive that led me to
undertake this new *Treatise on Accompaniment*,[4] I
could add here a summary of the materials contained
therein, & say a word about the order I observed in

writing it; but it is better to refer the Reader to p. ii
the Table of Contents, where he will see at a glance
the layout of the entire work.

However, it perhaps would not hurt to anticipate
several objections that might arise in this Treatise. Why, after having established the Fourth both
as a consonance & as a dissonance, have I not explained the circumstances when it is a consonance &
when it is a dissonance? Why have I not formulated
a specific Rule addressing the manner of resolving
dissonances, since most Teachers of Accompaniment
teach their Students to resolve them? Why have I
put one Flat more than is customary in all of the
Tonalities [i.e., key-signatures] that are in the
minor Mode?[5]

My response to the first two objections is that
they concern the Rules of Composition, & not those
of Accompaniment. *Refer to* the Treatises of Nivers,
Masson, & others;[6] and also to the Dictionary of
Music by Mr. de Brossard.[7] I have, however, not ne-
glected teaching the resolution of dissonances--in
discussing the movement of the hands in Chapter V,
Rules 8 & 9 [pp. 60-61]. As for the Flat [i.e., the
extra flat in minor flat key-signatures]: it is absolutely necessary, because all Tonalities in the
minor Mode have the Sixth from their final as essentially minor.[8] It is for this reason that the Flat
must be put by the Clef [i.e., in the key signa-
ture], & not in the course of the Air [i.e., the
melody] as an accidental--as it is usually done;[9]
this is a significant error that has not been yet
recognized to the present time.

With regard to the Examples that I have given for
each Rule, I have tried to make them into as many
brief Preludes in which the chord in question might
be found in the three possible arrangements it may
have.[10] This perhaps will have forced the Modulation
[i.e., the melodic and harmonic progression] in several places; but in order to follow a more regular
one [i.e., a *modulation* that conforms to the rules],
it would have been necessary to extend overly each
example.[11] I have even been sometimes obliged to
abandon that commitment [*assujettissement*], because
it would have led me too far afield, & then Students
would have been more bewildered than enlightened.

Finally, the Rules contained in this Treatise may be practiced on all Instruments of several Parts [i.e., harmony instruments], but particularly on Keyboard Instruments--which are the most suitable & the most commonly used for Accompaniment.

A NEW TREATISE
ON ACCOMPANIMENT
WITH THE HARPSICHORD

CHAPTER ONE

DEFINITION OF ACCOMPANIMENT

[DEFINITION DE L'ACCOMPAGNEMENT]

Accompaniment is the Art of playing the Thorough-bass on the Harpsichord, or on some other Instrument.[1]

It is called *Accompaniment*, because while playing the Bass one must join other Parts with it to form chords & harmony.[2]

These Parts are added following certain principles & rules, which will be the subject of this Treatise on Accompaniment.

One cannot understand the principles of Accompaniment without first having a distinct idea of the nature of Music.

Music is a mixture of various agreeable sounds [*sons*] whose sweetness, combination & arrangement delight the soul--entering it by way of the sense of hearing.

One pitch is [heard to be] different from another when it is brighter & sharper, which is said to be *higher*; or when it is deeper & graver, which is said to be *lower*.

Since the Harpsichord contains all of the pitches involved in the construction of works of Music, it is easy to tell the differences between them by striking all of the keys (*touches*) one after another; for if one begins from the left & plays [a glissando] toward the right, one will find that the pitches become increasingly higher (that is, they become brighter [*s'éclaircissant*]); & if one begins at the right & plays [a glissando] toward the left,

one will find that they become increasingly lower
(that is, deeper).[3]

The difference or the distance that exists from a
low pitch to a high pitch is called an *interval*.
One uses this term because one pitch is regarded as
being farther away from another when it ascends into
the treble [*au dessus*] or descends into the bass [*au
dessous*]. In fact, if one takes into account the
layout of the Keyboard, the keys that produce the
brightest pitches are the farthest away from those
that produce the deepest pitches.

Intervals have different names, according to
whether they are larger or smaller: that is, according to whether there is more or less distance from
the low to the high pitches--or, to say it better,
there are as many different intervals as there are
different distances between a low pitch & all the
various pitches ranging varying heights above it.

The smallest of all the intervals is called a
semitone: it is the interval found between two
pitches very close to one another, as between *mi* &
fa--which are so close that there is no other pitch
between them.

Although *fa* & *sol* as well as several other notes
on the Keyboard might be close neighbors to one another, I do not call that [interval] *very close* because there is another pitch between the two--the
Sharp of *fa* (which is closer to *fa* than is *sol*, &
which is closer to *sol* than is *fa*).[4]

All of the keys of the Keyboard, including the
white ones with the black,[5] are separated from each
other by the interval of semitone.

> From *ut* to its Sharp there is a semitone.
> From the Sharp of *ut* to *re*, a semitone.
> From *re* to the Flat of *mi*, a semitone.
> From the Flat of *mi* to *mi*, a semitone.
> From *mi* to *fa*, a semitone.
> From *fa* to its Sharp, a semitone.
> From the Sharp of *fa* to *sol*, a semitone.
> From *sol* to its Sharp, a semitone.
> From the Sharp of *sol* to *la*, a semitone.
> From *la* to the Flat of *si*, a semitone.
> From the Flat of *si* to *si*, a semitone.
> And finally from *si* to *ut*, a semitone.

These semitones are of different types; but this
distinction is not necessary [i.e., relevant] in
Accompaniment.[6]

The more wide-spread intervals have other names,
which we will discuss in the course [of this trea-
tise] after we have completed the concepts of Music
that we give here.[7]

In the composition of pieces of Music one makes
use more frequently of the seven pitches called *ut,
re, mi fa, sol, la, si,* than one does the five other
pitches included under the names of Sharps & Flats.
It is for this reason that in the arrangement of the
keys on the Keyboard the seven keys *ut, re, mi, fa,
sol, la, si* are positioned more conveniently for the
hand than are the Sharps & Flats; and it is also for
this reason that in Musical Tablature each of these
seven pitches [*sons*] are placed on a specific degree, while the other ones have none at all.[8]

Since the seven pitches *ut, re, mi, fa, sol, la,
si* are used more frequently than the other ones
[i.e., the sharps and flats], in the principles of
Music they are considered as if they were the only
ones involved in the composition of pieces. Thus in
the course of this Treatise we will always establish
our rules with reference to these seven pitches, &
we will call them *the seven notes of Music*--because
they are usually known under this name & concept.[9]   p. 3

Since the notes of Music are of varying heights,
they are rightly regarded as the degrees [i.e., the
lines and spaces] upon which the *melody* walks [*des
degrez sur lequels le chant se promene*], by raising
and lowering itself almost continually.[10]

If the note *ut* is taken for the first degree,
then the note *re* will be the second [degree], the
note *mi* the third, the note *fa* the fourth, & so
forth for the rest: this is fully explained in the
first chapter of the *Principles of the Harpsichord*.

But if one were to take some other note for the
first degree, as, for example, the note *sol*: then
the note *la* would be the second degree, the note *si*
the third, the note *ut* the fourth, & so forth for
the rest.

A note which is on the second degree from another
is called in Musical terms (i.e., in music terminology) *the Second* of that first note; that note which

is on the third degree is called *its Third*, that note which is on the fourth is called *its Fourth*, etc.[11]

Thus, if *ut* is taken as the first note & as the fundamental Pitch [*Son fondamental*]: then *re* [in relation to *ut*] is the *Second*, *mi* the *Third*, *fa* the *Fourth*, *sol* the *Fifth*, *la* the *Sixth*, *si* the *Seventh*, the second *ut* the *Octave*, the second *re* the *Ninth*, the second *mi* the *Tenth*, etc.

If one takes the note *re* as the fundamental Pitch & as the first degree: then *mi* [in relation to *re*] is the *Second*, *fa* the *Third*, *sol* the *Fourth*, *la* the *Fifth*, etc.

The various distances that are possible between one pitch and another, as I have already said, are called *Intervals* in terms of Music & of Accompaniment; & the entire science of Accompaniment consists of just the knowledge & the practical use of these Intervals.

ON THE INTERVALS

[*DES INTERVALLES*]

In Music, or rather in Accompaniment, we recognize only eight different intervals, which are:

The Second,	such as	*ut* to *re*.
The Third,		*ut* to *mi*.
The Fourth,		*ut* to *fa*.
The Fifth,		*ut* to *sol*.
The Sixth,		*ut* to *la*.
The Seventh,		*ut* to *si*.
The Octave,		*ut* to the second *ut*.
And the Ninth,		*ut* to the second *re*.

Example [1]

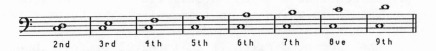

Most Intervals divide into four types, called *major, minor, diminished, & augmented.* Some others divide into only three types, called *perfect, dimin-* p. 4 *ished, & augmented* [*juste, diminuée, & superfluë*]. But since the distinctions that might be made among all of the various types of each Interval have little bearing on the rules of Accompaniment, we will speak here just of the ones [i.e., the types of each interval] that absolutely must be known in order to understand the rules of this Art.

There are two types of Seconds: the *minor* Second & the *major* Second.

The minor Second is an interval of a semitone: as from *mi* to *fa*, or from *si* to *ut*.

The major Second is an interval of a tone: as from *ut* to *re*, from *re* to *mi*, etc.; examples of it are given below.

When one speaks of the Second in terms (i.e., the terminology) of Accompaniment, one always means the major Second--because that is the only one used [in accompaniment].

There are two types of Thirds: the *major* Third and the *minor* Third.

The *major* Third is an interval of two tones: as from *ut* to *mi*, from *fa* to *la*, etc.

The *minor* Third is an interval of a tone & a semitone: as from *re* to *fa*, from *mi* to *sol*, etc.

There are two types of Fourths: the *perfect* Fourth, & the *major* or *augmented* Fourth, commonly called the *Tritone*.

The perfect Fourth is an interval of two tones & a semitone: as from *ut* to *fa*, from *re* to *sol*, etc.

The Tritone is an interval of three tones: as from *fa* to *si*, etc.

When one speaks of the Fourth, one always means the perfect [Fourth].

There are three types of Fifths: the *perfect* Fifth, the *diminished* Fifth (commonly called the *false Fifth*), & the *augmented* Fifth.

The perfect Fifth is an interval of three tones & a semitone: as from *ut* to *sol*, from *re* to *la*, etc.

The false Fifth is an interval of two tones & two semitones: as from *si* to *fa*, etc.

The augmented Fifth is an interval of four tones: as from *ut* to *sol-sharp*, from *mi-flat* to *si-natural*, etc.

There are two types of Sixths: the *major* Sixth, & the *minor* Sixth.

The major Sixth is an interval of four tones & a semitone: as from *ut* to *la*, from *re* to *si*, etc.

The minor Sixth is an interval of three tones & two semitones: as from *mi* to *ut*, from *la* to *fa*, etc.

There are three types of Sevenths: the *major* Seventh, the *minor* Seventh, & the *diminished* Seventh.

The major Seventh is an interval of five tones & a semitone: as from *ut* to *si*, etc.

The minor Seventh is an interval of four tones & two semitones: as from *ut* to *si-flat*, from *re* to *ut*, etc.

The diminished Seventh is an interval which encompasses in its width three minor Thirds: as from *ut-sharp* to *si-flat*, from *sol-sharp* to *fa-natural*, etc.

There is only one type of Octave, which is the *perfect* Octave.

The perfect Octave is an interval of five tones &
two semitones: as from *ut* to *ut*, from *re* to *re*,
[etc.].

There are two types of Ninths: the *major* Ninth, &
the *minor* Ninth.

The major Ninth is an interval of six tones & two
semitones: as from an *ut* to the second *re* above;
from a *re* to the second *mi* [above], etc.

The minor Ninth is an interval of five tones &
three semitones: as from a *mi* to the second *fa*
above, from a *si* to the second *ut* [above], etc.

The nature & various types of each interval   p. 5
having been explained (as we have just done), the
student of Accompaniment now should seek out for
himself all of the intervals from each note or key
on the Keyboard, & all of the various types [of each
interval]; & he should become so adept at this that,
for whichever key one might show him, he could say
immediately which other key forms the major Third,
or minor [Third], or the Fourth, or the Tritone, or
the Seventh, etc.[1]

And in order to facilitate learning this, we will
set forth here in music notation all of the intervals that are used in Accompaniment.

In all of the following Examples, the single
Notes are those which cannot have the Intervals in
question--except in a few very rare instances of
which it is not yet time to speak.[2]

DEMONSTRATION OF THE INTERVALS,
*in all of the manners in which they are found
on the Keyboard.*

Major Seconds alone used in the Accompaniment

Major Thirds

Minor Thirds

p. 6

Fourths

Tritones

Fifths

False Fifths

Augmented Fifths

p. 7

Major Sixths

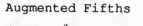

Minor Sixths

Major Sevenths

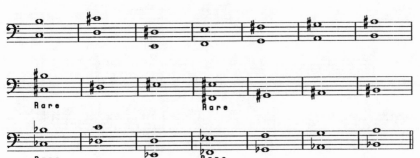

Minor Sevenths

Diminished Sevenths

Octaves

Major Ninths

Minor Ninths

When two or more pitches sounded at the same time strike the ear agreeably, this assemblage of pitches is called a *Consonance*; if this assemblage shocks the ear instead of delighting it, it is called a *Dissonance*.

Now, of the various intervals of which we have just spoken, there are some in which the upper note forms a consonance with the lower note, & others in which it forms a dissonance.

The intervals in which the upper note forms a consonance with its bass are:

      The Octave,
      The Fifth,
      The Fourth, which sometimes also acts as a dissonance,
      The Thirds (either major or minor),
      The Sixth (either major or minor).

Those [intervals] in which it forms a dissonance are:

      The Second of all types,
      The Tritone,
      The false Fifth,
      The augmented Fifth,
      The Seventh of all types,
      The Ninth, also of all types.

All Consonances are not equally sweet, nor are all Dissonances equally strident. The precise examination of their true qualities will form the subject of a lengthy Dissertation that I plan to write some day;[3] but this [examination] is not at all necessary here, because it is more important for students of accompaniment to know how to use the intervals than [for students] to know whether in fact they are sweet Consonances or strident Dissonances. p. 9

With regard to the intervals, there are two important remarks to be made.

The first: having decided on a note as the fundamental pitch of an interval, when one speaks of the Third, of the Fifth, or of some other interval of that note, one always means the Third above, the Fifth above, etc., & never the Third or the Fifth below. Thus if the note *ut*, for example, were taken as the fundamental note: its Third is the *mi* above, & not the *la* below; its Fifth is the *sol* above, & not the *fa* below. In a word, intervals are always calculated above the note that serves as their fundamental pitch, & never below it.

The second remark is: [because] intervals that exceed the span of the Octave (such as the Ninth, the Tenth, the Eleventh, etc.) are only the repeti-

tion of those intervals within the [span of the] Octave, they do not count for what they are in reality
[i.e., compound intervals], but rather as those
[intervals] of which they are just the repetition
[i.e., simple intervals]. That is to say, the Ninth
is counted as the Second (except for a special case
which we will explain below),[4] the Tenth is counted
as the Third, the Eleventh as the Fourth, & so on
for all the other [compound] intervals, however far
away they might be from their fundamental note.

Thus, for example, with regard to the first *ut* at
the bass end of the Keyboard, the first *mi* following
it ascending is its Third, the second *mi* naturally
[i.e., by its nature] is its Tenth, the third *mi* its
Seventeenth, & the fourth *mi* its Twenty-Fourth;
nonetheless, in the terms of Accompaniment each one
of these *mi*s are treated like the Third from this
first *ut*--because they are just [Octave] repetitions
of one another.

It is the same for all the other intervals; this
is why when in the course of this Treatise we speak
of intervals, it does not necessarily mean just the
absolute intervals (that is, those intervals within
[the span of] the Octave), but also those beyond it
which are [Octave] repetitions of the absolute in-
tervals--regardless of how distant they might be
from their fundamental note.

If, for example, I were to play the first *re* at
the bass end of the Keyboard, & I asked you to point
out the Fifth from this *re*: you would not be obliged
to play the first *la* above it, which is its absolute
Fifth. It would be enough for you to play any *la*
on the Keyboard; whichever one it might be, it would
always be the Fifth of my *re*.

If it were necessary to distinguish the intervals
taken within [the span of] the Octave from those
taken beyond it, one could name the first ones *absolute intervals*, & the others *double, triple,* or
quadruple intervals--depending on whether they might
be the first, the second, or the third [Octave] repetition of the absolute intervals.[5]

One could say, for example, that the first *mi* at
the bass end of the Keyboard is the *absolute Third*
of the first *ut*; that the second *mi* is its *double*

Third; that the third *mi* is its *triple Third;* &
finally that the fourth *mi* is its *quadruple Third.*

One could use the same terms to describe Fourths,
Fifths, & and all other intervals; but this distinction is not made in Accompaniment. The [Octave] repetition of intervals there are considered as [equi-
valent to the absolute] intervals themselves.

Exception for the Ninth

However, the Ninth (while being an [Octave] repetition of the Second) is not always treated as a
Second. There are some occasions when in reality   p. 10
one treats it as a Ninth, by giving it different
Accompaniments than those given when one considers
it just as a Second. This will be examined later
on.[6]

In the practice of Accompaniment, the Ninth is
considered (either the absolute Ninth, the double
Ninth, or the triple Ninth) as we have discussed it
for the other intervals.

CHAPTER III

ON THE PRACTICE OF ACCOMPANIMENT

[DE LA PRATIQUE DE L'ACCOMPAGNEMENT]

We said that Accompaniment is the Art of playing the Thoroughbass by combining other Parts, that is, other notes, [with the bass] to form chords & harmony. Now, it must be explained how this is done.

One plays the Bass with the left hand, & for each Bass note one strikes three other [notes] are supplied in the right hand--thereby forming a chord on each [bass] note.[1] However, one sometimes passes over Bass notes without giving them Accompaniment: but here is not the place to mention this (we will discuss it in Chapter VIII [pp. 101-102). However it should be pointed out that Thoroughbass notes are of two types: some are *simple* [i.e., unfigured], and others are *figured*.

On a simple [bass] note one plays for accompaniment what is called the *perfect* or *natural* chord--composed of the Third, the Fifth, & the Octave above this [bass] note. So for the accompaniment of an *ut* one plays a *mi*, a *sol*, & an *ut*. For the accompaniment of a *re*, one plays a *fa*, a *la*, & a *re*.

Example [2]

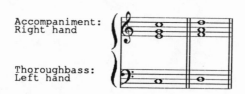

Accompaniment: Right hand

Thoroughbass: Left hand

(It is like this for all of the other [bass] notes.)

There is no specific order to retain in the arrangement of the notes of the chord: the Third may

be the lowest of the three, as in the above example;
or it may be in the middle; or it may be on top; &
accordingly, the Fifth & the Octave may also be
either on the bottom, in the middle, or on the top
of the chord.

What determines the arrangement of the parts is
the position of the hand playing the accompaniments   p. 11
[i.e., the right hand]: the rule is that once one
has placed his [right] hand on the Keyboard to play
the first chord of the Air[2] being accompanied, one
should then take all of the subsequent chords in the
closest position in which they are found; & following this rule requires the parts to change their arrangement with each chord played.

Example [3]

When a Bass note is figured, one no longer gives
it the Accompaniment of the perfect or natural
chord; rather, one gives it the interval indicated
by the figure, & the accompaniments applicable to
that interval. It is now necessary to explain the
meaning of the figures, & then we will discuss the
accompaniments given to them.

2 indicates the Second.
3 indicates the Third.
3*b* indicates the minor Third.
b without 3 also indicates the minor Third.
3*#* indicates the major Third.
without 3 also indicates the major Third.
4 indicates the Fourth.
4*#* or *#*4 indicates the Tritone.
4 intersected by an oblique line also indicates
the Tritone.
5 indicates the Fifth.
5*b* or *b*5 indicates the false Fifth.

5̸ intersected also indicates the false Fifth.

#5 indicates the augmented Fifth.

5# also indicates the augmented Fifth.

When 5# follows the false Fifth, it then only indicates the perfect Fifth.

6 indicates the Sixth.

6b or b6 indicates the minor Sixth.

6# or #6 indicates the major Sixth.

7 indicates the Seventh.

7b or b7 indicates [both] the minor Seventh & the diminished Seventh: because there is no special symbol for the latter, it is left up to the Accompanist to distinguish [whether the Seventh is minor or diminished].

7# or #7 indicates the major Seventh.

8 indicates the Octave.

9 indicates either the major or the minor Ninth.

There are six Remarks to make regarding the Figures of which we have just spoken.

First: the Figures in the Thoroughbass are usually placed above the [bass] notes to which they pertain, & sometimes below them--but never directly beside them.

Second: we call some symbols Figures that properly speaking are not Figures (such as b & #). However, they serve as Figures only when they are in the row of Figures--because, outside of [that row] they are just Flats and Sharps, as usual.

Third: a [bass] note is sometimes figured with just a single Figure, & other times it has several [figures] at the same time.

Fourth: several Figures pertaining to a single [bass] note are placed sometimes above one another, and sometimes beside one another.

Fifth: for a single [bass] note there are sometimes several Figures above one another as well as several [Figures] beside one another.

p. 12

Finally, sixth: the Figure is not always perpendicularly above its [bass] note, but sometimes a little to the side, & sometimes even quite far to the side--but always higher than [the bass note].

In the proper time & place we will point out everything that should be understood by these differences; but now I must discuss the accompaniments given to each Figure.

I. *Rules for the Accompaniment of [bass] notes figured with a single figure*

The Second is doubled & is accompanied with the Fifth when the following [bass] note descends by a semitone & is either figured with a 6 or else is not figured.

Example [4]

In the above instance, one could furthermore accompany the Second with a doubled Fifth.

Example [5]

The Second is accompanied with the Fourth & Fifth when the following [bass] note descends a semitone & is figured with a false Fifth.[3]

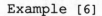

Example [6]

The Third is accompanied with the Fifth & Octave; this is called the *perfect* or *natural* chord, such as that one gives to unfigured [bass] notes.

p. 13

Example [7]

Whether the Third is indicated either simply by a 3 without distinction of major or minor, or is marked with major or minor indicated by a 3 combined with a Sharp or a Flat (as we have shown above in our explanation of the Figures) brings no change to bear in the accompaniment given to it: one always accompanies it with the Fifth & Octave.[4]

I will not tell you here why the Third is sometimes indicated simply by a 3, & sometimes by a 3# or a 3*b*. This involves an acquaintance with the *modes*, of which it is not yet time that I instruct you.

The # by itself on a Bass note signifies the perfect chord, with the major Third.

The *b* by itself also signifies the perfect chord, but with the minor Third.

The Fourth is accompanied with the Fifth & Octave.[5]

Example [8]

The Tritone is accompanied with the Second & Sixth when the following [bass] note descends by a tone or by a semitone.[6]

Example [9]

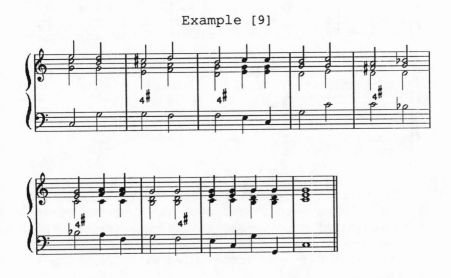

One could replace the Second with the Octave in the Accompaniment of the Tritone: however, the Second is more commonly used there than is the Octave.

The Tritone is accompanied with the Octave & the   p. 14
Sixth when the following [bass] note descends a Fourth, is accompanied with a perfect chord, & falls on the first beat of the measure.

Example [10]

The Tritone is accompanied with the Third & Sixth when the following [bass] note descends a semitone, is accompanied with a perfect major chord, and falls on the first beat of the measure.[7]

Example [11]

The Fifth is accompanied with the Third & Octave. This is the perfect chord, such as one gives to un-figured [bass] notes. See the example for the Third [ex. 7].

The false Fifth is accompanied with the Third & Sixth.

Example [12]

The false Fifth is accompanied with the Third & Octave, like the perfect Fifth, when the following [bass] note (instead of rising a semitone like it usually does) moves by a larger interval--either descending or ascending.[8]

Example [13]

*Source lacks f'.

The augmented Fifth is accompanied either with the Second & major Seventh, or (which is the same thing) with the major Seventh & major Ninth.[9]

Example [14]

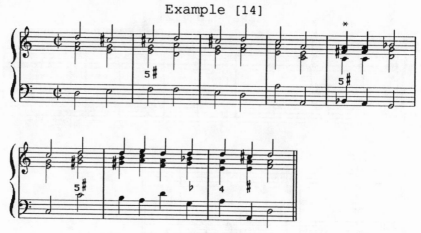

*Source shows f' instead of f'#.

The Sixth 6 is accompanied with the Third & Octave.

Example [15]

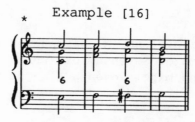

The Sixth 6 is doubled & is accompanied with the Third when the following [bass] note rises a semitone & has for accompaniment a perfect chord.

Example [16]

*Source has incorrect placement of treble clef.

The Sixth 6 is also accompanied with a doubled

Third when the following [bass] note rises a semitone & has for accompaniment a perfect chord.

Example [17]

These chords containing either two Sixths & one
Third, or else two Thirds & one Sixth, are called
doubled chords. Either one or the other is equally
correct for [bass] notes figured with a 6, provided
that the following [bass] note rises a semitone & is
accompanied with a perfect chord.[10]

Finally, the Sixth may also be accompanied with
the Third & Fourth.

Example [18]

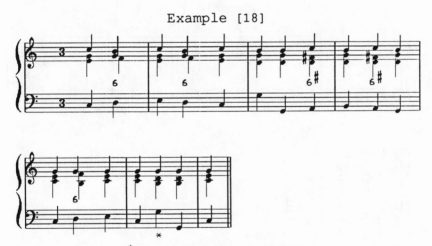

*Source shows B instead of G.

Since it is necessary to make distinctions among   p. 16
things to avoid confusion, we will give different
names to these various chords of the Sixth.

The first chord composed of the Third, Sixth, &
Octave will be called the *simple* chord [*l'accord
simple*], to distinguish it from those chords in
which one doubles a part.

The second chord containing two Sixths & one Third will be called the chord *doubled by the Sixth* [l'accord *doublé par la Sixiéme*].

The third [chord] which contains two Thirds & one Sixth will be named the chord *doubled by the Third* [l'accord *doublé par la Tierce*].

Finally, the fourth [chord] composed of the Third, Fourth, & Sixth will be called the *little chord* [*le petit accord*], because in fact this chord is closely-spaced [*peu étendu*] when the Third is on the bottom--as one may see in the preceding example.[11]

There are some instances when one should play the *simple* chord, others that require the *doubled* chord, & still others that demand instead the *little* chord. But we will speak of these instances when we discuss the choice of the chords in Chapter 6.

The Seventh (either major or minor) is accompanied with the Third & Fifth.

Example [19]

*Source has misplaced sharp the key signature.

Or else one accompanies it with the Third & Octave.

Example [20]

The Seventh is not accompanied as well with the
Third & Octave as it is with the Third & Fifth.[12]   It
is a sort of license to replace the Fifth there with
the Octave: one should do it only when one is forced
to. We will discuss in the chapter *Concerning the
Choice of the Chords* [p. 68-69, Rule 16] the circumstances that force one to do it [*la necessité qui
y force*].

The Seventh is accompanied with the doubled Third
when the preceding [bass] note is either a semitone
or a tone lower than the one having the Seventh, and
has for its accompaniment a perfect *major* chord
(that is, a perfect chord in which the Third is major).

Example [21]

This manner of accompanying the Seventh occurs   p. 17
only after a major chord in which the Third was
the highest of the three Parts, as in the above
Example.[13]

The diminished Seventh is accompanied with the minor Third & false Fifth.

Example [22]

The figure alone does not tell us if the Seventh is diminished or if it is just minor: this is for the Accompanist to decide for himself. He can do so only if he has learned the Modes: but it is still not yet time to speak of them.

The Octave 8 is accompanied with the Third & Fifth. This is the perfect chord, for which we do not give an Example here. *See* [the Example] for the Third on page 13 [p. 24, ex. 7].

The Ninth 9, when it is major, is accompanied with the Third & Fifth; & when it is minor, with the Third & Seventh.[14]

Example [23]

The figure does not tell us if the Ninth is major or minor; the Accompanist must decide this for himself.

II. *Rules for the Accompaniment of [bass] notes figured with two figures*

When we speak here of [bass] notes figured with two figures, we mean that these two figures are placed above one another (so as to assign to their [bass] note two separate intervals at the same time), & not beside one another--for that would indicate something else, which we will examine a few pages further on.

Since two parts of the chord are already determined by the figures, the Accompanist has only to add the third [part]; & here are the Rules for doing it.

The double figure Two & Four $\frac{4}{2}$ is accompanied with the Fifth--or, if one wishes, with the Sixth, but the Fifth is preferable.[15]

Example [24]

p. 18

The double figure Two & Tritone $\frac{4\sharp}{2}$ is accompanied with the Sixth.

Example [25]

The double figure Three & Five $\frac{5}{3}$ is accompanied with the Octave. This is the perfect chord. *See* the previous article on the Third above, page 13 [p. 24].

The double figure Three & Six $\frac{6}{3}$ is accompanied with the Octave. This is the *simple* chord of the Sixth [i.e., $\frac{8}{6}$]. *Refer* above, to the article on the Sixth, page 15 [pp. 28-30].[16]

The double figure Three & Seven $\frac{7}{3}$ is accompanied with the Fifth. This is the same accompaniment as the [single-figure] Seventh. *See* the article above, page 16 [pp. 30-31].

The double figure Three & Eight $\frac{8}{3}$ is accompanied with the Fifth. This is the perfect chord demonstrated above, page 10 [p. 20].

The double figure Four & Five $\frac{5}{4}$ is accompanied with the Octave.

Example [26]

The double figure Four & Six $\frac{6}{4}$ is accompanied with the Octave.

Example [27]

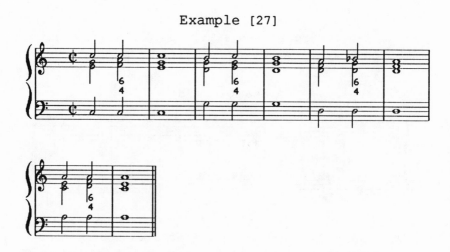

Notice that when a [bass] note thus has Four & Six $\frac{6}{4}$, the Sixth should always be of the same kind

[*nature*] as the Third was in the preceding chord.
That is, if the Third of the preceding chord was
major, then the Sixth [of the present chord] should
also be major. And if the Third [of the preceding
chord] was minor, then the Sixth [of the present
chord] should also be minor. The above Example
illustrates this for you.[17]

The double figure Tritone and Six $\overset{6}{4}\#$ is accompan- p. 19
ied with the Octave.[18]

Example [28]

etc.

The double figure Four & minor Seventh $\overset{7b}{4}$ within
the cadence (explained later [pp. 44-46]) is accompanied either with the Fifth or with the Octave.

Outside of the cadence, it is accompanied with
either the Octave or with the Ninth.[19]

Example [29]

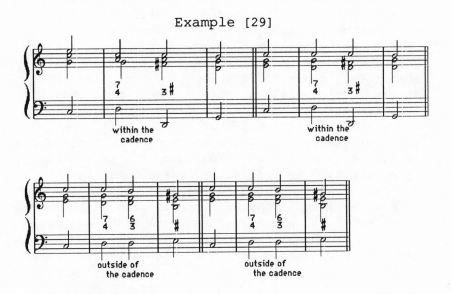

The double figure Four & Nine $\frac{9}{4}$ is accompanied either with the Seventh or with the Fifth.[20]

Example [30]

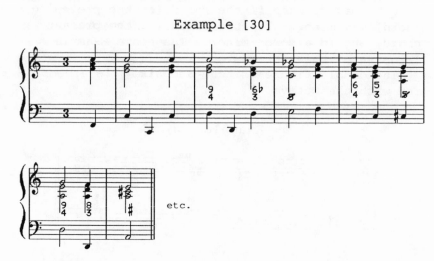

Monsieur Charpentier, in his Opera *MEDÉE*, uses the figure Nine & Eleven $\frac{11}{9}$ instead of Four & Nine $\frac{9}{4}$.[21] But [these two figures mean] the same thing, since the Eleventh is just the [Octave] repetition of the Fourth. It is with little necessity that he figures Eight & Ten $\frac{10}{8}$ instead of Three & Eight $\frac{8}{3}$, which indicates the same chord.[22] Any interval that is just the repetition [i.e., the compound interval] of another does not need to be figured precisely as it is: instead of [the compound interval], it is much better to figure the simple interval.[23] To present an Accompanist with figures that he is not accustomed to seeing is a useless bother--particularly when these [compound] figures only indicate what others [simple figures] more commonly used indicate just as well [by themselves].

Of all the intervals that are [Octave] repetitions of others, the Ninth alone must be figured [as it is]--for, in its function [*qualité*] as a Ninth it is accompanied in a different manner than is the Second, of which it is the [Octave] repetition.

Moreover, it is the Bass progression that determines whether a particular interval is to be [treated] as a Ninth or as a Second. The only time that a Ninth occurs is on a Bass note that ascends, whereas

the Second may occur either on a [bass] note that
remains on the same degree as the preceding [bass
note], or on one that descends a tone. *See* the   p. 20
Examples of the Second & of the Ninth, pages 12 & 17
[pp. 23-24, exx. 4-6 and p. 32, ex. 23].[24]

   The double figure Five & Six $\frac{6}{5}$ is accompanied with
the Third.

Example [31]

   The double figure false Fifth & Six $\frac{6}{\flat 5}$ is accompanied with the Third. This is the chord of the
[single-figure] false Fifth. *See it* in the above
Example, page 14 [p. 27, ex. 12].

   The double figure augmented Fifth & Seven $\frac{7}{5\sharp}$
is accompanied with the Ninth. This is the chord of
the [single-figure] augmented Fifth, demonstrated
above, page 15 [p. 28, ex. 14].[25]

   The double figure augmented Fifth & Nine $\frac{9}{5\sharp}$ is
accompanied with the Seventh. This again is the
augmented Fifth chord demonstrated above, page 15.

   The double figure Five & Seven $\frac{7}{5}$ is accompanied
either with the Third or with the Octave. These are
the same chords formed on the [single-figure] Seventh. *See them* in the above Examples, page 16 [pp.
30-31, exx. 19-21].

   The double figure Five & Eight $\frac{8}{5}$ is accompanied
with the Third. This is the perfect chord demonstrated above, page 13 [p. 24, ex. 7].

   The double figure Five & Nine $\frac{9}{5}$ is accompanied

either with the Third, or else by doubling the
Fifth.

Example [32]

The double figure Six & Eight $^8_6$ is accompanied
with the Third. This is the *simple* chord of the
Sixth [i.e., $^6_3$], of which we have spoken above on
page 15 [pp. 28-30].
    The double figure Seven & Nine $^9_7$ is accompanied
with the Third.[26]

Example [33]

    Instead of accompanying Seven & Nine with the
Third, one could give to the [bass] note having
these two figures the same chord as the preceding
[bass] note. That [chord] is nearer at hand, &
sometimes even more agreeable to the ear.[27]

p. 21   Example [34]

III.   On [bass] Notes figured with a triple figure

I call [bass] notes figured with a triple figure those that have three figures above one another.

The only rule to follow with regard to these kinds of [bass] notes is to give them for accompaniment the very intervals indicated by the three figures they have, without adding anything else [i.e., any other chord tones] to them.

Example [35]

IV.   On [Bass] Notes that have several figures beside one another

When a [bass] note has several figures beside one another, one assigns it several consecutive chords; & one assigns it as many [consecutive chords] as there are successive figures--by means of reducing the duration of each [chord] in proportion to the increasing number [of chords], as the following Example will illustrate.

These figures are more often double than simple, & sometimes they are even triple [figures].

Example [36]

[Example 36 cont.]

With regard to the duration of each chord, it is calculated as I have said by the number [of chords] there are divided into [*comparé avec*] the value of the [bass] note bearing them. But some discernment is needed in order to determine whether they should be equal or unequal in duration. Those who are experienced determine this by the long or short notes of the solo Part [*la Partie chantante*],[28] because these chords are but made to follow it. If Copyists wished to be precise, they could easily indicate [how long the chords should last] by arranging their figures in such a way that their positions would make it clear on which beats of the measure they [the chords] should sound--as I have done in the above Example. That would determine their duration precisely. But this is what they so often fail to do, either out of ignorance or carelessness; nevertheless it is the sole means of determining this duration, & we should make it a fundamental Rule of Musical Tablature [i.e., musical notation], as we have [already] done for the shape & the position of the notes [on the staff]. But I strongly doubt that Musicians give it much consideration, for I see many other things even more necessary than this to establish or to reform in Music--of which, however, not much thought has yet been given at all.

p. 22

Until this shortcoming [*deffaut*] is corrected, we will try to compensate for it by the following Rules.

Usually, a Thoroughbass note seldom has more than two successive figures. Thus, with only two chords to play on this [bass] note, it is easy to determine that each [chord] should have half of its duration. If [the bass note] is a Whole-note, each chord will have the duration of a Half-note. If it is a Half-note, each will have the duration of a Quarter-note, & if it is a Quarter-note, each will have [the duration] of an Eighth-note.

If there are four chords to play on a Whole-note,
each of them will be assigned the duration of a
Quarter-note; & for a Half-note, each of them will
be assigned the duration of an Eighth-note.

If there are three chords on a Whole-note, the
first [chord] will be assigned the duration of a
Half-note, & each of the other two [chords] the duration of a Quarter-note; or, on the contrary, the
first two [chords will be assigned] the duration of
a Quarter-note, & the third [chord] the duration of
a Half-note. One can determine this by listening to
the solo Part [*la Partie chantante*], or by reading
it [from the score] if it is in front of him.

If there are three chords to be played on a
dotted Half-note, each will last a Quarter-note.

If there are just two [chords to be played on a
dotted Half-note], the first [chord] will last a
Half-note, & the second [chord] a Quarter-note; or,
on the contrary, the first [chord] will have the
value of a Quarter-note, & the second [chord] that
of a Half-note. One determines this by the tempo
[*mouvement*] of the Air.

Finally, without further belaboring this point,
you should consider that for a Bass note whose value
can always be divided into two, three, or four equal
portions, one can adjust the number of figures to
this division--since it is easy to see by their number, by the solo part [*le Chant*], & by the tempo
[*mouvement*] of the Air whether each [chord] should
have for its duration a quarter, or a half, or
three-quarters, or one-third, or two-thirds of the
[total value of the bass] note.

I vow that these Rules are vague & little capable
of satisfying you if you wish to have this matter
settled absolutely: but do not blame me for this,
for it is the fault of those who have not precisely
positioned the figures.

Sometimes for a [bass] note having just a single
figure (either simple, double, or triple), this
figure is not found directly above its [bass] note
but rather a little toward the right, as in the following example. In that case one gives this [bass]
note two successive chords: first the perfect chord,
followed by the chord denoted by the figure.

Example [37]

If the figure is far to the side of its [bass] note, as in the second Measure of the above example, this indicates that the first chord should be much longer than the second. This is self-evident in the example.

p. 23   Also in the case of the preceding example, sometimes instead of a single figure one encounters several [figures] in succession. When this happens, after [playing] the perfect chord one plays as many other chords as there are successive figures--determining the duration of each [chord] by the number [of figures], by the value of the [bass] Note that bears them, by the solo part [*le Chant*], & by the tempo [*mouvement*] of the Air.

After the enumeration that I have given in this Chapter of all the chords (both consonant and dissonant) of Music (but for which I have provided nearly all examples on *Ut* & on *Re*[29] so as not to enlarge this volume needlessly), you should now learn them for yourself by heart on all the other [bass] notes of the Octave as well as on the Sharps & Flats [i.e., on all twelve notes]. You will not be able to accompany at sight [à *livre ouvert*] unless you know [the chords] in this way on all bass notes & in their three arrangements, as I have described them.

V.   *Reduction of figured Chords to perfect Chords*[30]

Those who are learning Accompaniment usually have more difficulty understanding & remembering by heart figured chords than [they do] perfect chords. But it is easy to make this less difficult, by pointing

out that when a [bass] note has several figures that
assign to it an unusual chord--this chord, (though
unusual for that [particular bass note]) is often
the perfect chord of another [bass] note. When an
Ut, for example, is figured with a 6, the chord denoted by 6 on *Ut* is the perfect chord on *La*; if it
is figured with Four & Six $\frac{6}{4}$, this is the perfect
chord on *Fa*; if it is figured with 7, or with $\frac{7}{5}$, or
with $\frac{5}{3}$, this is the perfect chord on *Mi*, etc.

In order, therefore, to give the Reader all possible assistance on the above matter, I am going to
teach him how to imagine the majority of dissonant
chords indicated by these figures as perfect chords.

The accompaniment of a [bass] note figured with
Two, Four, & Six $\frac{6}{4}{2}$, is the perfect minor chord of its
Second.

When the [bass] note has just Two & Four $\frac{4}{2}$, or 2
alone, one could still give it the minor chord of
its Second--even though I have taught the opposite
in speaking of these figures earlier.[31]

The accompaniment of a [bass] note figured with
Two, Tritone, & Six $\frac{6}{4\#}{2}$ is the perfect major chord of
its Second. We call the major chord the one with
the major Third, & the minor chord the one with
minor Third.

When the [bass] note has just Two & Tritone $\frac{4\#}{2}$, or
else Tritone & Six $\frac{6}{4\#}$, or else the Tritone alone $4\#$,
its accompaniment would always be the major chord of
its Second.[32]

The accompaniment of a [bass] note figured with
a 7, or with Five & Seven $\frac{7}{5}$, or with Three, Five, &
Seven $\frac{7}{5}{3}$, is the perfect chord of its Third.

The accompaniment of a [bass] note that has Four
& Six $\frac{6}{4}$, or else Four, Six, & Eight $\frac{8}{6}{4}$, is the perfect
chord of its Fourth.

The accompaniment of a [bass] note that has Five,
Seven, & Nine $\frac{9}{7}{5}$, is the perfect chord of its Fifth.

The accompaniment of a [bass] note figured with
a 6, or with Three & Six $\frac{6}{3}$, or with Three, Six, &
Eight $\frac{8}{6}{3}$, is the perfect chord of its Sixth, or [the
perfect chord] of the *Third below* [*sa sous-tierce*]
--which is the same [bass] note.

The accompaniment of a [bass] note that has Four
& Seven $\frac{7}{4}$, or Four & Nine $\frac{9}{4}$, or Seven & Nine $\frac{9}{7}$, or

Four, Seven, & Nine $\frac{9}{7}$, is the perfect chord of the [bass] note one tone ^{4} lower.[33]

The other figures cannot be re-evaluated as perfect chords [of other bass notes].

VI.   On the Cadence

In addition, as I have said, to knowing by heart all chords imaginable on all the keys of the Keyboard, it is furthermore good to know how to play on each one [i.e., on each key] the progression called the *Cadence*.

The Cadence is a melodic ending [*termination de chant*] that one can consider as the conclusion of a musical phrase or period: for, as I have shown in the *Principles of the Harpsichord*, Music has periods & phrases just like speech.[34]

In the Cadence, the Bass usually ends its melodic line [*chant*] with three notes--of which the second [note] is an Octave lower than the first, & the third [note is] a Fourth higher than the second [note].

The usual accompaniments of the Cadence are: on the first [bass] note, the Fourth accompanied with the Fifth & Octave; on the second [bass note], the major Third accompanied with the Fifth & Seventh; and on the third [bass note], the perfect chord.

Example [38]

Sometimes the Bass ends its melodic line with only two notes--of which the second [note] is a Fifth lower than the first [note], or else a Fourth higher (which amounts to the same thing). Then, if the first [bass] note is long in value, one usually gives it the two chords that would have been played on the first two [bass] notes of the three-note Ca-

dence; & if [the first bass note] is short, it has
for accompaniment only the perfect major chord.

Example [39]

There are five types of Cadences in Music,
namely:

> The perfect Cadence,
> The interrupted Cadence [*La Cadence rompuë*],
> And three types of imperfect Cadences.

The perfect Cadence is the one in which the Bass
ends its melodic line with two or three notes in the
manner that has just been shown in the two examples
above.[35]

The interrupted Cadence is one in which the last
[bass] note turns away from the ending [*chute*] that
would naturally conclude its melody in order to take
an ending [*termination*] that does not conclude at
all.[36]

Example [40]

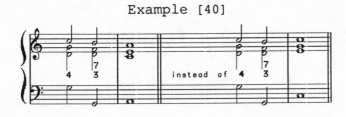

With regard to the three types of imperfect Ca-   p. 25
dences: since we will have an opportunity to speak
of them towards the end of this Book, we will post-
pone explaining them here--since it is not necessary
that you learn about them at this time.[37] However,
there are still a few observations to be made on the
Cadence.

First: when one speaks of the Cadence in general,
one always means the perfect Cadence.

Second: the Cadence takes the name of the note on
which the Bass ends. Thus, when one speaks of a

Cadence in *Ut* or in *G Sol Ut*, that means a Cadence in which the Bass ends with an *Ut* approached from a *Sol*.[38]

Third: the Cadence is not always figured in the Score [*dans les Livres de Musique*], & often the Accompanist must recognize it solely by the progression of the [bass] notes; but that is not difficult after one has had a little practice.

Fourth and last: regardless of whether the [bass] notes of the Cadence are figured or not, one should always give them the chords that I have indicated in the above examples--except that instead of the Seventh that I nearly always add in the penultimate chord, one may instead play the Octave. Nevertheless, the Seventh is much better there--but take care not to forget that in the penultimate chord the Third must always be major.

We will have further opportunities to speak of the Cadence later on.[39]

ON TONALITY, MODE, AND TRANSPOSITION

[DES TONS, DES MODES, ET DE LA TRANSPOSITION]

He who wishes to accompany on any kind of Instrument should have at least a superficial understanding of the Tonalities & the Modes of Music.

Every Air or Musical Piece is composed in a particular tonality [ton] & in a particular mode.[1]

The tonic note [ton] of an Air is the note on which it ends; & that note is also called the *final*.

If the final of an Air is an *Ut*, one says that the Air is composed in *C Sol Ut* (this is the term).[2] If [the final] is a *Re*, then it is in *D La Re*, etc.

When an Air has several parts [i.e., voices], the parts (even the one called the Theme [*le Sujet*])[3] sometimes end on a note other than the essential final [*la finale essentielle*] of the Air;[4] but as for the Bass--whether it might be the theme of the Air or not, it will always end on the essential final. So when one wants to know in which tonality [*sur quel ton*] an Air is composed, one should look to the final [note] of the Bass. This final [bass note] is always the fundamental note of the Air, &, so to speak, the *Tonic* note.

The Mode is the determination of the course [*determination du chemin*] that the melody [*le chant*] of an Air & its parts (when it has them) must stay on-- all with respect to the final note. This is what establishes the species of each interval; it is the particular system upon which a Musical Piece is built.

There are just two Modes in Music: the major Mode & the minor Mode.

The Mode of an Air is major when the Third, Sixth, & Seventh from the final or tonic note are major.

The Mode is minor when the Third, Sixth, & Seventh from the final are minor.

The Second, Fourth, Fifth, & Octave are of the same species in the major Mode as in the minor

[Mode]; so the difference between the two Modes consists entirely of the difference in the three intervals indicated above [i.e., the Third, Sixth, and Seventh].

This is perhaps not all that might be said on the Modes of Music if one wished to discuss the subject thoroughly. But one should at least say this much about them when one discusses just Accompaniment.

The tonality & the mode of an Air are two absolutely inseparable things, & one can never speak of the first [i.e., the tonality] without at the same time expressing the second [i.e., the mode]--or at least without implying it; for if one says, for example, that an Air is in *G Re Sol*, this indicates that [the Air] proceeds along the pitches [*cordes*] of a modulation[5] of which the final is a *Sol*; but this does not say whether the modulation is major or minor. It is therefore necessary to add one or the other of these terms, & to say that [the Air] is in *G Re Sol* major mode, or in *G Re Sol* minor mode.

There are, nevertheless, some modulations that are self-implied--because they are considered to be natural to particular tonalities.

When one says that an Air is in *C Sol Ut* without mentioning its modulation, one implies that it is major.

When one says that [an air] is in *D La Re*, one implies that its mode is minor.[6]

p. 27   When one speaks of *E Si Mi*, one supposes the minor mode.

In speaking of *F Ut Fa*, one supposes the major mode.

G Re Sol has no modulation more natural to it than another. Thus one always has to state the mode when one speaks of an Air in *G Re Sol*.

A Mi La is assumed to have the minor mode.

B Fa Si-Natural, a tonality in which one rarely composes, has no modulation that might be assigned specifically to it (though if it had one, it would be minor). But by popular custom, when one says that an Air is in *B Fa Si* one means that it is in *B Fa Si-Flat* [i.e., B♭] & its modulation is major.[7]

When an Air does not conform to this usual practice (that is, when it is not in one of the above tonalities, modified [i.e., with the mode applied]

as described here) one never speaks of its tonality
without at the same time specifying its modulation.
Thus when an Air is in *C Sol Ut* & its mode is not
major, one does not fail to state the mode--by
saying *C Sol Ut minor mode*, or *C Sol Ut minor*.

If [an Air] is in *D La Re* & its modulation is not
minor, then one says that it is in *D La Re major
mode*, or *D La Re major*.

Some Musicians, instead of using the terms *major*
& *minor* to specify the mode of an Air, make use of
the older terms *Becarre* [i.e., natural] & *Bemol*
[i.e., flat].[8] In order to indicate, for example,
that an Air is in *C Sol Ut minor Mode*, they say that
it is in *C Sol Ut Bemol*; in order to indicate that
another [Air] is in *D La Re major Mode*, they say
that it is in *D La Re Becarre*, & so forth for the
others; but these expressions [i.e., *Becarre* and
Bemol], which are perhaps more common, nevertheless
are not as appropriate as the others [i.e., major
and minor].

The division of the Octave into twelve parts as
we do it, while giving us twelve different pitches
(each of which can be taken for the *Tonic* note of an
Air), enables us to say that we have twelve tonalities [*tons*] in our Music--thus using the word tonality in the sense that we gave it at the beginning of
this Chapter. And at the same time one can see that
it is possible to have just exactly twelve [tonali-
ties], since the Octave can be divided into just
twelve parts.[9]

However, because nine of the twelve pitches that
derive from this division of the Octave can each be
considered in two different ways,[10] this multiplies
the number of tonalities to twenty-one; but these
twenty-one tonalities are in name only, because in
reality there exist only twelve.[11]

The following Demonstration illustrates all of
these tonalities; and because there are several
that, as I said, are the same [tonalities] under
different names, I have indicated those that are
identical to one another with corresponding Letters.

Among these tonalities there are some more commonly used than others. There are even several
[tonalities] that perhaps have never been brought
into play [*mis en oeuvre*];[12] but I wished to omit

none from the Demonstration--because the majority of our Composers, by now using many [tonalities] not previously in use, may finally render them all equally commonplace.[13]

Take note, if you will, that some tonalities require all of the notes of the Octave to be marked with a Sharp [*Dieze*] or with a Flat [*Bemol*], & that there might even be several notes doubly marked [i.e., marked with double-sharps and double-flats]. For easier recognition of notes having double-Sharps and double-Flats, I have separated the single-Sharps and single-Flats from the double-Sharps and double-Flats by a bar drawn between them. In addition, I have indicated with numerals the number of Sharps or Flats each tonality requires. The following Demonstration illustrates all of this.[14]

p. 28   *Demonstration of the Tonalities & Modes*

The Tonalities for which the words major and minor are omitted are the common Tonalities--for which the Mode is usually implied. The Modes [for the Tonalities lacking indication of major or minor] are as listed below.

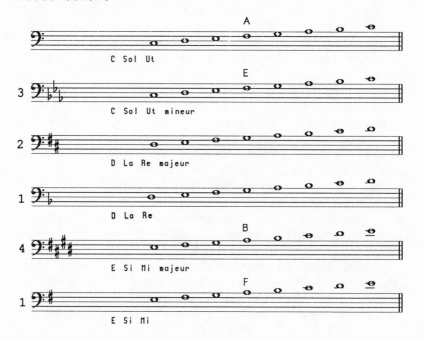

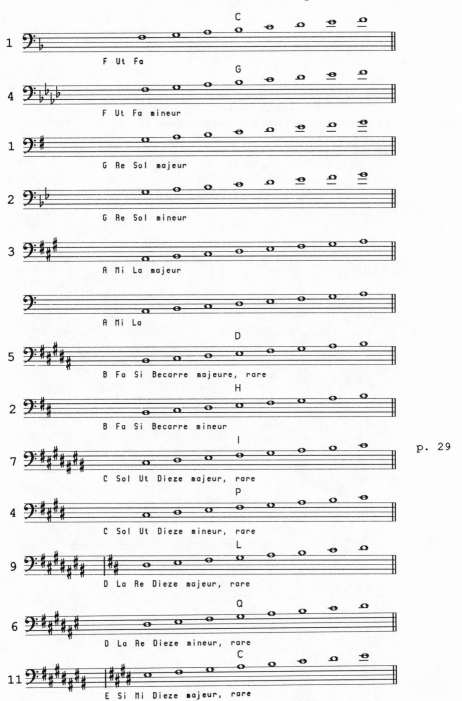

p. 29

p. 30

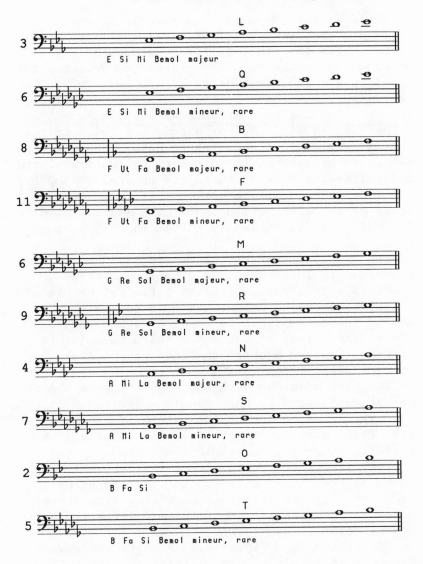

3 E Si Mi Bemol majeur

6 E Si Mi Bemol mineur, rare

8 F Ut Fa Bemol majeur, rare

11 F Ut Fa Bemol mineur, rare

6 G Re Sol Bemol majeur, rare

9 G Re Sol Bemol mineur, rare

4 A Mi La Bemol majeur, rare

7 A Mi La Bemol mineur, rare

2 B Fa Si

5 B Fa Si Bemol mineur, rare

Since the Mode in a Piece of Music is what establishes the species of each interval & is what deter-   p. 31
mines the pitches [*cordes*] (that is, the sounds
[*sons*]) of which the Piece should be composed; before accompanying an Air one should examine its
Tonality & Mode to determine which pitches [*cordes*]
pertain to it, so as to derive accompaniments from
these particular pitches [*cordes*] & not from others
--unless in the course of the Piece one is directed
to change some [pitches] by means of a Sharp

[*Dieze*], a Flat [*Bemol*], or a Natural [*Becarre*],
which are the symbols designated for this purpose.

Supposing then that an Air is composed in *C Sol
Ut major Mode*: the natural pitches [*cordes*] for this
tonality are the seven notes *Ut, Re, Mi, Fa, Sol,
La, Si*--without Sharp or Flat on any pitch. Thus,
when playing the Bass of such an Air [and when] accompanying an *Ut*, a *Fa*, or a *Sol*, the Third in the
chords [*accords*] of these three notes should always
be major--because it is so due to the nature of the
Mode (likewise [the Third in the chords] of *Re, Mi,
La, & Si* is naturally minor). Therefore, one should
never play a minor Third on *Ut* or a major [Third] on
Re--unless it is expressly marked in the Thorough-
bass.

The change [*mutation*] of the major Third to minor
is marked in Thoroughbasses either by a three
combined with a Flat 3*b*, or by a Flat alone placed
on [i.e., above or below] the note for which this
change [*changement*] is to be made; & the reverse
change [*mutation*] of the minor Third to major is
marked either by a three combined with a Sharp 3*#*,
or by a Sharp alone.

The Flat combined with any Figure lowers the interval designated by that Figure a semitone; if this
interval is major due to the nature of the Mode,
[the Flat] makes it minor; if [this interval] is
perfect, [the Flat] makes it diminished.

Conversely, the Sharp widens the interval designated by the Figure to which it is attached by a
semitone: if [the interval] is minor, [the Sharp]
makes it major; & if [the interval] is perfect, [the
Sharp] makes it augmented.

If, following a Figure with a Flat, the same
Figure immediately should be repeated with a Sharp,
this [Sharp] serves to cancel the Flat; and conversely, if following a Figure with a Sharp the same
Figure should be repeated with a Flat, this [Flat]
serves to cancel the Sharp.[15]

When the Figure is simple (that is, without Flats
or Sharps), one plays the interval that it naturally
requires, as determined by the Mode.

What we have just said shows that Accompaniments
sometimes deviate from the pitches [*cordes*] of the
Mode to take on foreign ones [i.e., pitches outside

of the mode]: but an Accompanist should never do
this unless it is specifically indicated in the
Thoroughbass.

The Bass [part] also sometimes makes this change
[*changement*] by taking on (as do the accompaniments)
a Sharp, a Flat, or a Natural; and with regard to
this, one should take note that no interval (except
for the Octave) becomes altered along with the Bass
when it [the Bass] takes on a pitch [*corde*] foreign
to the Mode. Thus, when *Ut* [in the Bass], for example, takes on a Sharp: the *Mi* (which is its Third &
is naturally major) still remains the Third of the
Sharp [i.e., the sharped Bass note] & becomes a minor Third by this change of the Bass. When *Si* [in
the Bass] takes on a Flat, the *Sol* (which is its
Sixth, & is naturally minor) similarly stays the
Sixth of *Si-Flat* & becomes by that [change in the
Bass] a major Sixth. For it is an inviolable rule
in accompaniment that, while the lower note of an
interval might change pitch [*change de corde*] in ascending or descending a semitone by means of a Sharp
or Flat, the upper note however (except when it
forms the Octave) must never change unless specifically indicated. As for the Octave [above the
Bass]: it always follows the change in the Bass (its
fundamental note) by becoming Flat or Sharp, according to what occurs [in the Bass]; nevertheless, p. 32
you will see in the following Rules that when any
Bass note takes on a Sharp, one no longer includes
the Octave in its accompaniment.[16] Therefore, the
exception of the Octave holds good only with regard
to Bass notes that take on a Flat.

Although we have said above that the accompaniments of an Air derive from the pitches [*cordes*] assigned to its Mode--nevertheless, the Fourth is not
taken when due to the nature of the Mode it happens
to be a Tritone instead of a true Fourth. Thus, in
the tonality of *C Sol Ut*, for example, when a *Fa*
happens to be figured with a four: one does not play
this Fourth on *Si-Natural*, but on *Si-Flat*--even
though this pitch [*corde*] is foreign to the Mode;
because *Si-natural* is the Tritone of *Fa*, & not its
perfect Fourth.

However, when due to the nature of the Mode the
Fourth of a [bass] note happens to be its Tritone

(as we have just shown), there are some Music Teachers who (to mark the Tritone on that note) figure it with just a simple four 4, & not with a sharped four 4# as one customarily does; this is why the Accompanist must then complete the sense a little [*un peu aider à la lettre*], & so to speak guess at the intention of the Composer. This is very easy to do after one has had a little experience: one determines [whether the Fourth is a perfect Fourth or is a Tritone] by the solo part [*la partie chantante*] (which almost always forms the intervals designated by the figures), or by the Bass progression (which always descends after a Tritone), or finally by the modulation--which alerts the sensitive ear to all that the [right] hand should play.[17]

Moreover, I am fully of the opinion that figures should always be written in this way; that is, one should not attach a Sharp or Flat to a Figure except when it is necessary to show that the interval must be played on a pitch [*corde*] foreign to the Mode; for (provided that the upper note of an interval does not deviate from the pitches [*cordes*] of the Mode) the figure does not need to indicate whether [the interval] is major, minor, diminished, or augmented; the state [*qualité*] of the lower note, together with the nature of the Mode, indicates this well enough without [the addition of a sharp or flat to the figure].

On Transposition

Transposition is the change that one makes when one takes an Air from the tonality in which it had been composed, so as to place it several Tones higher or lower in order to make it easier to sing or to play. If, for example, an Air had been composed in *C Sol Ut*, & if someone attempting to perform it in that tonality could not descend to the lowest notes of this Air, it would then be necessary to raise it a tone or two--by placing the *Ut* of this Air on *Re* or on *Mi*, & the other notes [raised] in proportion. If, on the contrary, someone could not reach the highest notes, the entire Air could be lowered by several degrees--by placing the *Ut* on *La*

or on *Sol*, & the other notes [lowered] in proportion. Thus, to transpose an Air is nothing more
than to take it from one tonality and to move it to
another--but without making any change to its Mode.

When one accompanies a voice that cannot accom-
modate the tonality [*ton*; i.e., range] of the Instrument being used to accompany, it then becomes
necessary to transpose or to tune [*accorder*] the Instrument to the range [*ton*] of the voice. But since
some Instruments cannot change tonality (such as
Flutes & all wind Instruments), & since most string-
ed Instruments used for accompanying would take too
long to retune [*racorder*], it is best for an Accompanist to know how to transpose.

In order to transpose readily, one imagines
notes under different names than those they natur-   p. 33
ally have; & to do this, one supposes a different
Clef than that which is actually there. Furthermore, this requires one to realize [*supposer*] sharps
or flats on particular degrees, depending on whether
one transposes it from a major Mode tonality to one
that is naturally minor, or, on the contary, from a
minor Mode tonality to one that is naturally major.
For example, if one transposed from *C Sol Ut* to *A Mi
La*, one needs to suppose three sharps--one on *Ut*,
another on *Fa*, & another on *Sol*: because *C Sol Ut*
has the third, sixth, & seventh [scale degrees] as
major; & since *A Mi La*, on the contrary, has them as
minor, it would not correspond to *C Sol Ut* without
these three sharps. If, on the other hand, one were
to transpose from *A Mi La* to *C Sol Ut*, one would
need to suppose three flats--one on *Si*, another on
Mi, & another on *La*: because *A Mi La* has the third,
sixth, & seventh [scale degrees] as minor, & the
intervals of *C Sol Ut* cannot correspond to it
without these three flats.

It is not necessary to say anything further on
this subject. A person who starts Accompanying is
not so inexperienced in Music that he cannot by himself make the necessary suppositions when he transposes from one tonality to another.

CHAPTER V

ON THE MOVEMENT OF THE HANDS

[DU MOUVEMENT DES MAINS]

There are in Accompaniment several rules to follow concerning the movement of the hands.

1. The first [rule is] that the hands should always move in contrary motion; that is, for an ascending Bass the accompaniment should descend, & for
a descending Bass the accompaniment should ascend.

One follows this [rule] in order to avoid a Part
from forming the Octave or Fifth against the Bass
twice in succession--which is absolutely forbidden.[1]

2. The second rule is that the right hand should
always take its chords in the closest position to
where they are found, & never seek [chords] far out
of position. Thus, the chords would be poorly cho-
sen if they were taken in the following order:

Example [41]

To accompany regularly [regulierement; i.e., ac-
p. 34 cording to the rules], one should choose [the
chords] in the following manner. [see Ex. 42]

Thus, in its chord progression the accompaniment
should always move by the smallest intervals pos-
sible--and sometimes not move at all [i.e., not
change chords] when the Bass permits this, as we
will see in the following Chapter [pp. 64-65, Rules
8-10].

Example [42]

3. The upper Part of the accompaniment should never ascend higher than the *Mi* of the last Octave of the Keyboard, or at the very most up to the *Fa*-- except when the Bass becomes Alto [*Haute-contre;* i.e., when the Bass part is notated with an alto clef], for then everything is placed in a high register [*car alors on monte tout fort haut*].[2]

4. When the Bass leaps by a large interval in the progression of its notes (in either ascending or descending motion), the two hands then may move in similar motion.

The large intervals are the *Fourth*, the *Fifth*, & all those that extend beyond.

The small intervals are the *Second* & the *Third*.

5. While approaching or leaving a doubled chord [i.e., $\frac{3}{3}$ or $\frac{6}{6}$], the two hands may move in similar motion--even when the Bass moves by just a small interval.

Example [43]

6. In the penultimate chord of a Cadence, if the note that forms the Third happens to be the highest of the three [in the right hand accompaniment], the following chord should ascend--regardless of whether the bass ascends or descends.

Example [44]

7. When the two hands happen to be so close to
each other that the right [hand] cannot play its
three-note chord without [forcing] the two hands to
rise at the same time, one then plays just two notes
--& the one of the three left out is the [note]
forming the Octave against the Bass.

Example [45]

After these accompaniments of just two notes, the
two hands may then move in similar motion; they are
sometimes even obliged to do so, as in the second
part of the above example--unless one were to play
several two-note chords in succession, which is also
permitted.

p. 35   8. After the Fourth 4, the false Fifth 𝄫, the
Seventh 7, & the Ninth 9, the accompaniment should
always descend--not necessarily all of the Parts,
but at least the Part that forms one of these four
intervals.[3]

Example [46]

9. After the Tritone 4#, the augmented Fifth 5#, the major Sixth figured 6#, & the major Seventh 7# when formed in passing on a Bass note that remains stationary, the accompaniment should ascend--either all of the Parts, or at least the [part] that forms any of these figures.[4]

Example [47]

If in the arrangement of the Parts that which forms the augmented Fifth happens to be either the lowest or the middle [Part], & not the highest (as shown above), one would descend to the following chord & not double it [i.e., & not play a doubled chord].

Example [48]

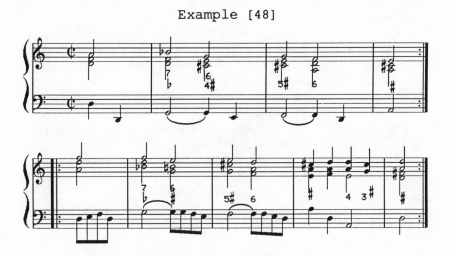

CHAPTER VI

ON THE CHOICE OF CHORDS

[DU CHOIX DES ACCORDS]

Since all chords, except those that are doubled, have in the arrangement of their notes three different orders (as we have shown above),[1] it often is left to the Accompanist to choose whichever order best pleases him. While special rules permit him in some instances to raise or to lower his [right hand] accompaniment (according to what he decides is appropriate), it is solely his good taste that determines all of this. He may even sometimes change the chords assigned to the [bass] notes when he decides that others are better suited. There are some [bass] notes for which the doubled chord works better than the perfect chord, others for which the simple chord of the Sixth works better than the doubled chord; this is left to the Accompanist to choose. He who chooses the best accompanies the most expertly.

1. For a Bass note of ample length, one may play two or three different chords successively, even though the score requires just one [chord]--provided that one feels that these chords will work with [*quadreront avec*] the solo Part [*la Partie chantante*].

2. On the contrary, one may sometimes entirely dispense with playing all of the chords indicated in the score when one finds that the [bass] notes are too overburdened [with figures].[2]

There are some [bass] notes that one may pass over without accompaniment, as we will discuss in the Chapter of the Licenses; there are also others that one must always accompany.[3]

3. One always accompanies the [bass] note that follows either a figured false Fifth ♭5, a Seventh 7, a Tritone 4#, or a major Sixth 6#.

4. One always accompanies the [bass] note that follows any dissonance, unless that dissonance were

to resolve on the same [bass] note that bore it--
that is, unless after the dissonance there might be
a consonant chord on the same [bass] note. The
Ninth 9, the Seventh 7, the augmented Fifth 5#, &
the Fourth 4 (treated as dissonances) are usually
resolved on the same note. *Look for* one [of these]
among the thousands of examples found in all musical
Scores.

   5. When the Bass moves either from a Flat [*un
Bemol*; i.e., a flatted note] to a Natural [*un Becarre*], or from an uninflected note [*une note naturelle*][4] to its Sharp [*un Dieze*]: one plays either a
doubled chord [i.e., $\frac{3}{6}$ or $\frac{6}{3}$] or else a false Fifth
on this Natural or Sharp.

Example [49]

6. But when [the Bass] moves either from a Sharp to
an uninflected note, or from a Natural to a Flat:
one either retains the doubled chord that the first
[bass] note had on the second [bass] note, or else   p. 37
one may play the simple chord of the Sixth [i.e., $\frac{8}{6}$]
on it; one is free to choose--but it is better to
retain the doubled chord.

Example [50]

*

*Source has misplaced treble clef.

   7. When a single [bass] note has two successive
chords, such as the perfect chord followed by either

the [chord of the] *Fourth* & *Sixth* or else the [sim-
ple chord of the] *Sixth*: this *Sixth* of the second
chord should be of the same type as the *Third* of the
first [chord]--that is, if the *Third* of the first
chord was minor, then the *Sixth* of the second
[chord] should also be minor; & if the *Third* was
major in the first [chord], this *Sixth* of the second
[chord] should also be [major].[5]

Example [51]

8. When the Bass has two consecutive notes, and
the second [bass note] is one degree lower than the
first: if there is a slur [*liaison*] from one [bass
note] to the other, then one retains the chord of
the first [bass note] on the second [bass] note.

Example [52]

The second of these two [bass] notes is usually
one tone lower than the first, as shown above; but
even if it were just a semitone lower, one would
still follow the same rule.
    9. All Bass notes contained under a slur should
pass under the accompaniment of the first [bass]
note [i.e., the first chord should harmonize all
slurred bass notes].[6] *See* Chapter 5 above, in the

Example of Rule 9 [p. 61, ex. 47].

10. When the Bass has two consecutive notes, and the second [bass note] is a tone lower than the first: [regardless of] whatever figures the second [bass] note has, it should be accompanied only by the chord of the first [bass note]--assuming that this first [bass note] had a perfect major chord.[7]

Example [53]

11. But if the first [bass] note had just a per-   p. 38
fect minor chord for accompaniment, and if there had been a Tritone in the figures of the second [chord], as shown above: in playing the [chord of the] second [bass] note it would be necessary to change the minor Third (of the first chord) to a major [Third].

Example [54]

12. If the Third of a Bass note (that is major, due to the nature of the Mode) happens to be figured minor in a particular passage, & if after this change [*mutation*] the same chord should be repeated several times (either immediately, or after a brief interruption): then one includes the minor Third in all of these repetitions--until such time that it might be refigured as major.

Example [55]

13. On the contrary, if [this Third] (that is minor, due to the nature of the Mode) happens to be figured as major in some passage, & is repeated several times after this change (in the manner that we have discussed above): then one includes [the major Third] in all of these repetitions--until such time that the figures restore it to minor.

Example [56]

The same [rule] is followed with regard to the other intervals.

14. When a Bass note takes on an accidental [*une feinte*] (that is, a Sharp, a Flat, or a Natural) & if either a moment before or after the same note became a part in the accompaniment, it should take on the same accidental as in the Bass; that is, if the Bass, while passing over, for example, an *Ut* Sharp, passed over a [bass] note (either a moment before or after) that should have had an *Ut* in its accompaniment, this *Ut* should be sharped there [i.e., in the accompaniment] as in the Bass, & not natural [i.e., uninflected]. And following the same rule, if the Bass (while passing over *Si Flat*) passed over a [bass] note (either a moment before or after) that should have had a *Si* in its accompaniment, this *Si* should be Flat there [i.e., in the accompaniment] as in the Bass, & not natural [i.e., uninflected] or Natural [i.e., with the inflection of a natural sign].[8]

Example [57]

For the Sharp & the Flat

p. 39

Remember this rule when you encounter accidentals in the Bass; one often breaks this [rule] by not paying attention.

15. When due to the nature of the Mode the intervals happen to be diminished or augmented instead of perfect, it is not necessary to change them to perfect unless this is expressly marked--because that would corrupt the Mode, which is never permitted.

The ear can accept falseness [*fausseté*; i.e., the diminished or augmented forms] of intervals when required by the Mode more than it can the corruption of Mode--even though this would reinstate the intervals to their perfect forms.

Example [58]
of Intervals false due to the nature of the Mode

The notes beside which there is a D form diminished
Intervals against the Bass; & the one beside which there
is an S forms an augmented [Interval]

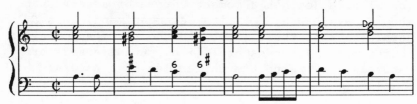

The ending of this example (from the last *La* of the Bass to the end) is one of the three types of imperfect Cadences, of which we have spoken in Chapter III, Article 6 [pp. 44-46].[9]

Notice that even though the intervals are left in the false forms in which the Mode places them, one still accompanies them as if they were perfect.

The chord following the *Little chord* [i.e., $\frac{6}{4}$] should always be like the one preceding it. *See* the last beat of the first entire measure of the previous example & the first beat of the second measure.

16. One must take care that a Part of the accompaniment does not form twice consecutively the Octave or the *perfect* Fifth against the Bass. This is avoided by following the rule of contrary motion cited in the previous Chapter [p. 58, Rule 1].

Example [59]

bad   7   good   7

As you can see, this rule makes it necessary to
accompany the Seventh with the Octave & Third, & not
with the Third & Fifth--as one should always do when
one is free to.

One nevertheless could accompany here the Seventh
with the Third & Fifth, by having all Parts descend
to the third chord in the following manner:

Example [60]   p. 40

7

But that could be tolerated only at a pinch [*mais
cela ne se pourroit souffrir qu'à toute rigueur*];
for the regularity [i.e., the rules] of composition
requires that the Part forming the Seventh against
the Bass may do so only by retaining the pitch
[*corde*] that it had in the preceding chord, which it
would not do if one had all Parts descend--unless
one imagined that the bottom [right-hand] Part stay-
ed on the same pitch, and the middle Part jumped
over it to become the lowest. This is called having
the Parts cross [i.e., voice crossing], & in fact it
is a permitted license--but one that should be used
only moderately.

17. One should furthermore take care that no Part
of the accompaniment should form an *improper progression* [*mauvaise progression*]--that is, it should
not sound two consecutive notes that the ear cannot
tolerate in succession.

The intervals that offend the ear in the progression of a part are *augmented Seconds, Tritones, &* all other augmented intervals of which we will say no more here--because the Accompanist has only to avoid the *augmented Second* and particularly the *Tritone*, since there is no risk of encountering the others if he follows the rule that advocates choosing chords in close position & near to each other [p. 58, Rule 2].

Since the Tritone was demonstrated earlier,[10] we have now to discuss only the augmented Second.

The augmented Second is an interval consisting of a *tone* & a *minor semitone*.

The minor semitone is the distance or interval between two adjacent pitches having the same name, as between a note and its Sharp or between a Flat [i.e., a flatted note] and its Natural [i.e., the same note with the inflection of the natural sign]; and the major semitone is the interval between two adjacent pitches having different names, as between *Mi* & *Fa*, or between *Ut Sharp* & *Re*, etc.

[Example 61]
Demonstration of the minor & major Semitones

minor Semitones

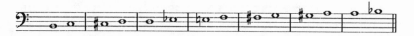

major Semitones

There are naturally just three augmented Seconds on the Keyboard: namely the ones on *Fa*, on *Si Flat*, & on *Mi Flat*.[11]

Example [62]

But in exceptional cases & in some transposed
tonalities, all minor Thirds on the Keyboard can become augmented Seconds--as you will easily realize
if you study the particular system of each tonality
as they are demonstrated above.[12]

One should therefore avoid the augmented Second   p. 41
in the progression of a single Part; & this requires
us to change the Accompaniments for some [bass]
notes--while always choosing suitable chords for
them, but not [necessarily the chords] one would
choose if there were nothing to avoid.

Thus, to avoid the augmented Second, one gives to
an unfigured [bass] note a chord doubled (by the
Third) instead of a perfect chord; & should it bear
a figure that requires a dissonance, one adds to
[this dissonance] only those consonances that permit
one to avoid the improper progression--& not those
[consonances] that ought naturally to accompany this
dissonance.

An Unfigured Example [63]

Because if one were to play a perfect chord on each
[bass] note, the upper Part of the accompaniment
would form the improper progression of a descending
augmented Second--since it would move from *Ut Sharp*
to *Si Bemol*.

Another Example [64] with the Seventh

Because if one were to accompany in this second manner, the middle Part would form an ascending augmented Second in its progression when moving from *Fa* to
Sol Sharp.

There are many people who make no scruple about
[including] improper progressions in the accompani-
ment--because they [i.e., the improper progressions]
are not very perceptible, & moreover one does not
always have time to avoid them while being carried
along by the measure.   There is even every reason to
believe that the Italians do not find them [i.e.,
improper progressions] shocking, since they often
use them explicitly--even in the very themes [*su-
jets*] of their Pieces.   One finds them in the *Son-
nantes* [i.e., sonatas] of the famous *Correlli*, now
so famous in Europe & so in fashion with us for the
past several years.   Thus you would not make a very
grave mistake should you allow yourself some improper progressions in the Parts of your accompani-
ment--provided that you do not make a mannerism of
them, and use them just by virtue of necessity.   I
would prefer, however, that one did not use them at
all, except for in particular highly unusual instances whereby one indeed feels that such negli-
gences are better than a more exact regularity
[i.e., strictly following the rules].[13]

18. When playing all chords in three notes [i.e.,
three notes in addition to the bass] one happens (by
the position of the hands) to be at risk of playing
consecutive Octaves or Fifths (in the manner in
which they are prohibited), one then leaves out [*re-
tranche*] a Part of the Accompaniment--thereby reducing it to two Parts; & the Part left out is that
which forms the Octave against the Bass.

p. 42

Example [65]

You can see that if one were to play the entire
chord on the third Bass note, one would play both
consecutive Fifths & Octaves at the same time--which
is avoided by leaving out a Part.

19. One furthermore leaves out a Part of the accompaniment when one realizes that by always playing
three [parts] one would inevitably fall into either
two Fifths or into an improper progression.

Example [66]

This leaving out of a Part is not strictly speaking an omission, but rather a uniting of two Parts
on a single pitch [*sur une même corde*]. For one
should imagine in the example given here that the *La*
& the *Fa Sharp* of the first chord both come together
on the *Sol* in the second [chord]; this is what I
tried to indicate by giving two stems to the note
Sol.

When our Bass note *Mi Flat* (here [in ex. 66] figured with a 7) has no figure at all, we would always leave out a Part in its accompaniment--or, as
one might prefer to understand it, we would unite
two [Parts] on a single pitch to avoid these very
mistakes [i.e., forming consecutive Fifths or an improper progression].

Example [67]

[Example 67, cont.]

or of

20. When the Bass has two consecutive notes ascending either by successive degrees [i.e., semitones and tones] or by interrupted degrees [i.e.,
leaps]: if the second [bass note] has two or three
figures at once (whatever they may be), one may
leave the chord of the first [bass note] on the
second [bass note].

Notice that I say that one *may* leave it there,
& not that one *must* leave it; because, although [the
chord of the first bass note] nearly always works
[on the second bass note], it may however sometimes
not work there at all. Nevertheless, it works so
much of the time that I would willingly make of it a
general Rule--since it is quite seldom that it is
found to be inadequate there [*s'y trouve de la def-
fectuosité*]; & should this come about, it would resolve itself [*se raccommoderoit*] so naturally to the
chord of the following [bass] note that I would have
no misgivings about leaving it there.[14]

21. When a single chord can serve several successive Bass notes, it is not necessary to change it.

p. 43

Example [68]

22. When moving from chord to chord, one should
examine to see whether several notes of the first
chord might be used in the next chord; & when this
is possible, it is not necessary to change these

notes. It often happens that two of the three notes
one has in hand can be used in the following chord;
therefore, one needs to change only one of them--but
the [note] that changes should move in contrary motion with the Bass.

Example [69]

23. One should never play two successive doubled
chords [i.e., $^6_3$ or $^3_6$] with either similar or contrary motion; but when a doubled chord can serve two
successive [bass] notes by changing only the note
that is not doubled, one can retain it.[15]

Example [70]

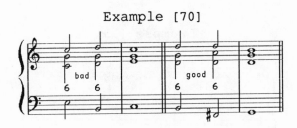

24. When in the Bass there are two consecutive
notes moving (either ascending or descending) by
successive degrees [i.e., semitones and tones], & if
they are each figured with a 6: one plays for each
of these notes the simple chord of the Sixth [i.e.,
$^8_6_3$].

Example [71]

25. If one cannot (or if one should not wish to) play the simple chord on each of these notes (which one is free not to do), then it is necessary to play chords of various types, while following these [rules]:

26. If the two Bass notes move in descending [motion], one can play on the first [bass note] a doubled chord [i.e., $\frac{3}{8}\frac{6}{3}$ or $\frac{6}{3}\frac{6}{6}$], & on the second the simple chord [i.e., $\frac{6}{3}$].

p. 44

Example [72]

Or else one can play the simple chord [i.e., $\frac{8}{6}\frac{}{3}$] on the first [bass note], & on the second the little chord [i.e. $\frac{6}{4}\frac{}{3}$].

Example [73]

But if the [bass] notes ascend, one should rather play the simple chord [i.e., $\frac{8}{6}\frac{}{3}$] on the first [bass note], & the doubled chord i.e., $\frac{3}{6}\frac{6}{3}$ or $\frac{3}{3}\frac{6}{6}$] on the second.

Example [74]

And if the second of the two [bass] notes is a semitone higher than the first, it is better to play the little chord [i.e., $\frac{6}{4}$] $\begin{smallmatrix}8\\3\end{smallmatrix}$ on the first [bass note], & the simple chord [i.e., $\frac{6}{3}$] on the second.

Example [75]

And finally, when the two Sixths are minor, & if after them the Bass ascends another semitone, one can play on the first [bass] note either the simple [i.e., $\frac{6}{3}$] or the doubled [i.e., $\begin{smallmatrix}3\\6\\3\end{smallmatrix}$ or $\begin{smallmatrix}6\\3\\6\end{smallmatrix}$] chord, & on the second [bass note] a false Fifth.

Example [76]

CHAPTER VII

RULES FOR DETERMINING THE FIGURES
when Thoroughbasses are Unfigured

[*REGLES POUR DEVINER LES CHIFFRES,*
quand les Basses-Continuës ne sont pas chiffrées]

Continuation of the choice of the Chords

Although it is customary to figure Thoroughbasses
in order to indicate the particular chords required
by the melodic theme [*sujet*] of each Piece, some oc-
casionally fall into the hands of Accompanists that
are not figured at all, or are figured inaccurately.
Thus if the figures are either left out or poorly
positioned, it is up the Accompanist to supply
through his own skill whatever may be missing on
the page.

In this Chapter we will discuss all of the figures that a Thoroughbass should have with regard to
its progression--so that, having understood the
Rules, the Reader might be able to correct by this
means all of the shortcomings [*deffectuositez*] found
in the Pieces presented to him.

1. A *Si*, a *Mi*, & a *Sharp* [in the bass] are always
presumed to be figured with a 6 & accompanied with
a doubled chord [i.e., $\frac{6}{3}$ or $\frac{6}{3}$], provided that the
following [bass] note ascends by a semitone & is
accompanied with a perfect chord.

Example [77]

2. One may include the Octave in the Accompaniment
of a *Mi*, a *Si*, or a *Sharp* [in the bass], when the

following [bass] note falls a major Third or moves
by some large interval in either ascending or descending. One absolutely must include [the Octave]
when this following [bass] note, when ascending by a
tone or a semitone, happens to be figured with a
Seventh.

Example [78]

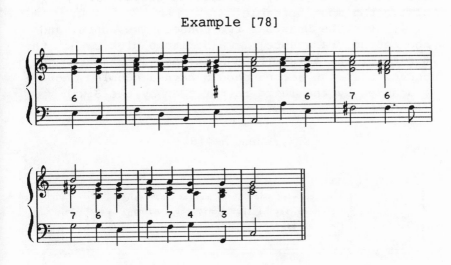

3. Every [bass] note is presumed to be figured
with a 6 & accompanied with a doubled chord [i.e., $\frac{3}{6}$
or $\frac{6}{3}$] when the following [bass] note ascends a semitone & is accompanied with a perfect chord. This
Rule is the same as the first [rule] of this Chapter.

Example [79]   p. 46

For both the preceding Rule & for the first one
of this Chapter, if one wishes he may use [for the
first bass note] the simple chord of the Sixth
[i.e., $\frac{8}{6}$] instead of the doubled chord; this is

allowed--but the doubled chord is safer for the
regularity [i.e., adherence to the rules] of the Accompaniment [*pour la regularité de l'Accompagnement.*

One may furthermore use the false Fifth there
instead of either the simple or the doubled chord;
but the latter [i.e., the doubled chord ⁶₃ or ³₆] is
always the most suitable.

4. When the Bass has two consecutive notes, and
the second [bass note] is a semitone higher than the
first: if the first [bass note] has a perfect major
chord, then the second should have a doubled chord--
& doubled by the Third rather than by the Sixth
[i.e., ³₆].

Example [80]

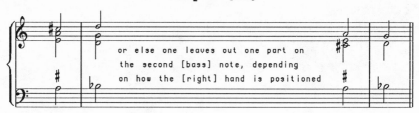

5. When the Bass has two consecutive notes, and
the second [bass note] is a semitone lower than the
first: if the second [bass note] has a major chord &
falls on the first beat of the measure, then the
first [bass note] should have a doubled chord [i.e.,
³₆ or ⁶₃]. This is the opposite of the preceding rule.

Example [81]

6. When the Bass has two consecutive notes, and
the second [bass note] is a semitone higher than the
first: if [the first bass note] has a major Sixth

figured 6#, then the second [bass note] should also
have a Sixth--which occurs naturally [i.e., through
the nature of the mode] as major [*laquelle se trouve
naturellement majeure*]. With regard to choosing
chords for these two [bass] notes, here is what must
be done: if one gives the simple chord [$^8_6_3$] to the
first [bass note], then one should give the doubled
chord [$^6_6_3$ or $^6_3_6$] to the second; & if one plays on the
first [bass note] the little chord [$^6_4_3$],then one
should play the simple chord on the second.

Example [82]

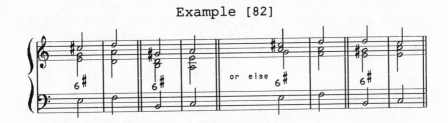
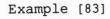

The choice between these two ways of accompanying
this [example] depends upon the position of the
[right] hand.
　　7. When the Bass has two consecutive notes, and　p. 47
the second [bass note] is a minor Third lower than
the first: if the first [bass note] has a perfect
minor chord, then the second should include the
false Fifth (instead of the perfect Fifth) in its
chord.[1]

Example [83]

　　8. A [bass] note should have the minor Third in
its chord when either the preceding [bass note] or
the one before it [*sa anteprécedente*] was this minor
Third.

Example [84]

*Original figure is 6.

9. [The bass note] should also have [the minor Third] when either the following [bass note] or the one following it [*sa subsuivante*] was this minor Third.

Example [85]

10. By a similar rule, a [bass] note should have the major Third in its chord when it is either preceded or followed immediately or closely thereafter [*immediatement ou mediatement*] by a [bass] note that forms this major Third.[2]

Example [86]

11. When the Bass has two consecutive notes, and
the second [bass note] is two tones lower than the
first: if the first [bass note] has a perfect major
chord, then it is necessary to play on the second
the simple chord of the Sixth [⁸₆₃].

Example [87]

p. 48

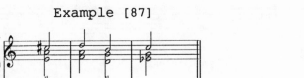

12. A [bass] note should have the false Fifth in
its chord (instead of the perfect Fifth) when the
Bass descends immediately or soon thereafter [*immediatement ou mediatement*] from a note that formed
this false Fifth.

Example [88]

13. When the Bass has two consecutive notes, and
the second [bass note] is either a Third higher or a
Sixth lower than the first: if [the first bass note]
has a perfect chord, then the second should have the
simple chord of the Sixth [⁸₆₃].[3]

Example [89]

*Diamond-shaped notes are *guidons* in source.

Another Example [90]

*Diamond-shaped notes are *guidons* in source.

Notice that wherever I speak of a *Third*, of a *Sixth*, or of any other interval without specifying its type, I mean by that all types in general.

14. When the Bass has three consecutive notes ascending by the interval of a tone, [as shown at letters] A and B, if the third [bass note] falls on the first beat of the measure [and] has for its accompaniment a perfect major chord, one must then realize [*supposer*] a 6 on the first [bass note], & on the second the double figure $^6_5$ accompanied with the minor Third.[4]

Example [91]

Even if the third [bass] note did not fall on the first beat of the measure, one nevertheless would give [all three bass notes] the same accompaniments [listed above].

p. 49

Example [92]

If there should be just the interval of a semitone between the first & second of these three [bass] notes [as seen below at letter] A, one could still give them the same accompaniments [listed above] instead of playing a doubled chord on the first [bass note], as we taught at the beginning of this Chapter [pp. 78-79, Rules 1 and 3].

Example [93]

But then the Third that accompanies the double figure $\overset{6}{5}$ must be major, because here the nature of the Mode determines it--as one can see by this last example.

Furthermore, these two ways of accompanying the three [bass] notes in the above example are both equally good; one can choose on that occasion whichever [accompaniment] one wishes--that is, whichever is most conveniently at hand.

15. When the Bass has three consecutive notes descending by successive degrees each the interval of a tone: if the first [bass note] has a perfect major chord, then the second [bass note] should have the same chord as the first & the third [bass note] the simple chord of the Sixth [$\overset{8}{\underset{3}{6}}$].[5]

Example [94]

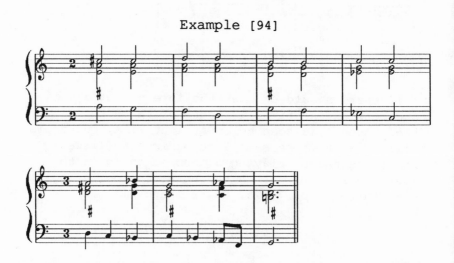

16. When the Bass has three consecutive notes descending by successive degrees: if the first [bass note] has a perfect chord & if the third [bass note] has a Seventh, then one gives to each of these three [bass] notes no other accompaniment than the perfect chord of the first [bass note]; however, one does not restrike the chord on the second [bass note]-- one holds it.

Example [95]

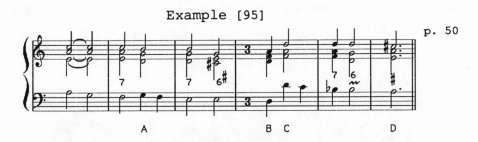

p. 50

In the above example there are two progressions [*passages*] that are two types of imperfect Cadences: the first from A to B, & the second from C to D.[6]

17. When the Bass has three consecutive notes--of which the second [bass note] is either a major or a minor Third lower than the first [bass note], & the third [bass note is] one tone higher than the second [bass note], has a perfect major chord for its accompaniment, & falls on the first beat of the measure: then one should realize [*supposer*] a 6 on the second of these three [bass] notes, & play there the simple chord of the major Sixth [$^8_6_3$].[7]

Example [96]

18. If the Bass has three consecutive notes--of which the second [bass note] descends a minor Third, & the third [bass note] reascends a semitone and falls on the first beat of the measure, then it is necessary to play:

On the first [bass] note, the perfect major chord,

On the second [bass note], either the simple

[b_6^8] or the doubled [b_6^3 or $_{b6}^{b6}$] chord of the minor
Sixth,
   And on the third [bass note], the perfect ma-
jor chord.[8]

Example [97]

19. When the Bass has three consecutive notes in
an intervallic order equivalent *to Mi, Ut, Fa*: if
the first [bass note] has a false Fifth, then the
second [bass note] should have a minor Seventh & the
third [bass note] a perfect chord. In this instance
the false Fifth is accompanied with the Third & Octave.

Example [98]

20. When the Bass has three consecutive notes--of
which the second [bass note] is a semitone higher
than the first, & the third [bass note is] either a
Fifth higher or a Fourth lower than the second [bass
p. 51 note] and falls on the first beat of the measure:

then it is necessary [to play] on the first [bass]
note a false Fifth [i.e., a *b*5 chord, as shown by ex.
99]; on the second [bass note] whatever perfect
chord occurs there, or else the simple chord of the
major Sixth [⁸⁶]; & on the third [bass note] the perfect major chord.

Example [99]

Three Bass notes in the above order form the con-
clusion of one of the three [types of] imperfect
Cadences, of which we have spoken in Chapter III,
Article 6 [pp. 44-46].[9]

21. When the Bass has three consecutive notes--of
which the first two are on the same degree [i.e., on
the same line or space], & the third [bass note] ascends a Fifth and falls on the first beat of the
measure: then one plays on the first & on the third
[bass note] the perfect chord, & on the second [bass
note] the simple chord of the major Sixth [⁸⁶, ap-
proached] with similar motion.[10]

Example [100]

Please note that whenever I speak of the perfect chord without specifying its type [i.e., major or minor], I always mean it to be whichever one the Mode assigns--as you can understand by the preceding example.

22. When the Bass has three consecutive notes--of which the first two are on the same degree [i.e., on the same line or space], & the third [bass note] descends a Fourth and falls on the first beat of the measure: if the first [bass note] has a perfect major chord, then the second [bass note] should have a Tritone [i.e., a #4̆ chord, as seen by Example 101], & the third [bass note should have] a perfect chord [approached] with contrary motion.

Example [101]

23. When the Bass has four consecutive notes ascending by an intervallic order equivalent to *Sol, La, Si, Ut*; if the last [bass] note falls on the first beat of the measure, & if each [bass note] is of sufficient value to warrant a chord, then one plays:

On the first [bass note], the perfect chord;

On the second [bass note], the minor Sixth in a simple [$b\frac{6}{3}$] or a doubled [$b\frac{6}{3}$ or $\frac{b6}{3}$] chord;

On the third [bass note], the false Fifth;

And on the fourth [bass note], the perfect chord.[11]

Example [102]

24. When the Bass has four consecutive notes descending by successive degrees, and the last [bass note] falls on the first beat of the measure: then one must take notice of where the interval of the semitone falls among these four [bass] notes. If it falls between the first & the second [bass] note, then one accompanies these kinds of progressions [*passages*] with:

On the first [bass] note, the perfect chord;

On the second [bass note], the doubled chord [$\frac{3}{6}$ or $\frac{6}{3}$];

On the third [bass note], the simple chord of the major Sixth [$\frac{8}{6}$] or else the little chord [$\frac{6}{4}$], depending on whichever is found nearest at hand;

And on the fourth [bass note], the perfect major chord.

Example [103]

If the second [bass] note moves by more quickly than the others, one can leave the chord of the first [bass note] on it by holding [the chord] without restriking it.

Example [104]

If the semitone falls between the second & the third [bass] notes, & if the first [bass note] has a perfect major chord, then one plays:

On the second [bass note] the Tritone, Second & Sixth;

On the third [bass note] the simple chord of the major Sixth [i.e., $\frac{8}{6}$];

And on the fourth [bass note] the perfect minor chord.

Example [105]

If the first [bass note] has a perfect minor chord, then one plays:

On the second [bass note] the Second, Fourth, & Sixth;

On the third [bass note] the little chord [$\frac{6}{4}$];

And on the fourth [bass note] the perfect minor chord.

p. 53

Example [106]

Finally, if the semitone occurs between the third & the fourth [bass] note, then it is necessary to play:

On the first [bass note], the perfect minor chord;

On the second [bass note], the perfect major chord;

On the third [bass note], the chord doubled by the Third [$\frac{3}{6}$];

And on the fourth [bass note], the perfect major chord.

Example [107]

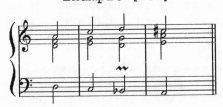

Or else, without changing the Accompaniment that
we have just assigned to the first & fourth [bass]
notes, one can give the second [bass note] the same
chord as the first, & the third [bass note] the
little chord [$\frac{6}{4}$]--in which case it must be noted that
[in the little chord] the Third is major, & the
Fourth is a Tritone.

Example [108]

If the second [bass] note happens to be short [in
duration] & if the third [bass note] is much longer:
then one could pass over the second [bass note]
without accompanying it [*sans accompagnement par-
ticulier*] & give two consecutive chords to the third
[bass note]--that is, first a Seventh [$\frac{7}{5}$] & then the
little chord [$\frac{6}{4}$], as in the preceding example, or
else [a Seventh chord and then] the doubled chord [$\frac{3}{6}$
or $\frac{6}{3}$].

Example [109]

In these kinds of progressions [*passages*], one always plays a trill [*tremblement*] on the [bass] note that has two chords; but one plays it only while taking the second chord--as is shown by the example above.[12]

All of the examples of the preceding rule, with slight differences among them, are types of imperfect Cadences of which we have spoken in Chapter III, Article 6 [pp. 44-46].[13]

p. 54   25. When the Bass has five consecutive notes descending by successive degrees--with the last [bass note] falling on the first beat of the measure & with each [bass] notes being of sufficient length to warrant a chord: if the first [bass note] has a major chord & if the intervallic order of these [bass] notes are equivalent either to *Sol, Fa, Mi, Re, Ut,* or to *La, Sol, Fa, Mi, Re,* then one plays:

On the first [bass note], the major chord;

On the second [bass note], the Tritone & its accompaniment [i.e., a #$\frac{6}{4}$ chord];

On the third [bass note], the doubled chord [$\frac{3}{6}$ or $\frac{6}{3}$];

On the fourth [bass note], the simple chord of the major Sixth [$\frac{8}{6}$];

And on the fifth [bass note], the perfect chord.

Example [110]

*Source shows e' instead of f'.

Depending on what is most convenient for the [right] hand, one could play on the third [bass] note the simple chord [$\frac{8}{6}$] & on the fourth [bass note] the little chord [$\frac{6}{4}$]--while retaining on the others [i.e., on bass notes 1, 2, and 5] the chords that we have indicated for them.

Example [111]

The examples of this Rule [illustrate] again one of the three types of imperfect Cadences.[14]

26. Although some progressions [*passages*] similar to those of the two preceding Rules might not end on the first beat of the measure (as they do in the examples of these Rules), one would still accompany them just as we have indicated.[15]

Example [112] for Rule 24

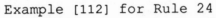

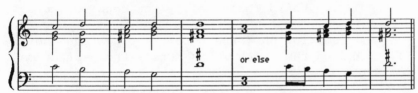

Example [113] for Rule 25

[Example 113 for Rule 25 cont.]

27. When the Bass has five consecutive notes as-
p. 55 cending by successive degrees--with the last [bass
note] falling on the first beat of the measure, &
with each of the [bass] notes being of sufficient
length to warrant a chord: if their intervallic order is equivalent either to *Ut, Re, Mi, Fa, Sol,* or
to *Re, Mi, Fa, Sol, La,* then one plays:

On the first [bass] note, the perfect chord;

On the second [bass note], the simple chord of
the major Sixth [$\frac{8}{6}$];

On the third [bass note], the doubled chord [$\frac{3}{6}$
or $\frac{6}{3}$];

On the fourth [bass note], the perfect chord;

And on the fifth [bass note], the perfect major
chord.

Example [114]

Or else, depending on what happens to be the most
convenient for the [right] hand, one plays:

On the first [bass note], the perfect chord;

On the second [bass note], the little chord [$\frac{6}{4}$]

On the third [bass note], the simple chord [$\frac{8}{6}$];

On the fourth [bass note], the Fifth & the
Sixth accompanied with the Third;

And on the fifth [bass note], the perfect major
chord.

Example [115]

This manner of accompanying these progressions [*passages*] to me seems preferable to the first one [i.e., to that shown in Example 114].

28. In the progression [*passage*] called *Çadence*, one always realizes [*suppose*] a 4 [i.e., a $\frac{5}{4}$ chord, as can be seen by the example] on the first of the three [bass] notes that comprise it, & a 7 on the second [bass note].[16]

Example [116]

29. If the Cadence consists of just two [bass] notes, and the second [bass note] either descends a Fifth or ascends a Fourth: then one plays two chords on the first [bass note]--provided that it is long enough to carry them.

Example [117]

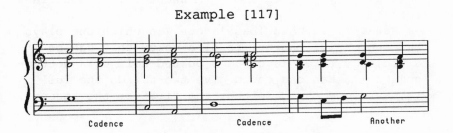

[Example 117 cont.]

Another

*Source shows d' rather than c'.

p. 56   30. In a Cadence composed of just two [bass] notes, if the first is not long enough to carry two perfect chords in succession, one then gives it just the perfect major chord--for which one sometimes replaces the Octave with the Seventh, depending on what one finds most convenient for the [right] hand.

Example [118]

Cadence   Cadence

31. When one plays two successive chords on a single [bass] note (either in a Cadence or else-where), each [chord] should last half the value of the [bass] note that carries them--as the above examples should make clear. *Refer back* to what we have already written above in Chapter III, Article 4 [p. 41].

However, if this [bass] note (on which one plays two successive chords) is of a value that can be divided by three (such as a dotted-half or a dotted-quarter), then one could give two-thirds the full value to one chord (either the first or the second).

Example [119]

32. When the [bass] note can thus be divided by three, then one can play three successive chords instead of two--with the first [chord] having a Fourth [i.e., a $\frac{5}{4}$ chord], the second being a perfect major [chord], & the third [chord] having a Seventh [i.e., $\frac{7}{5}$].

Example [120]

33. Even when the Cadence is composed of just two [bass] notes, the Accompanist may substitute three; but since this involves the licenses rather than the realization [*supposition*] of the Figures, we will reserve speaking of it until the following Chapter.[17]

CHAPTER VIII

ON THE LICENSES THAT ONE MAY TAKE IN ACCOMPANYING

[DES LICENCES QU'ON PEUT PRENDRE EN ACCOMPAGNANT]

Continuation of the choice of Chords

Having established the general Rules of Accompaniment in the preceding Chapters, we will now discuss some of the exceptions to these general Rules--that is, some of the Licenses that one may take in accompanying.

The first Rule that we proposed in Chapter III [p. 20] for the practice of Accompaniment is that *one should play a chord on each [bass] note*; but now we will say that:

1. When the Bass notes move by consecutive degrees, one is not obligated to accompany them all. One may accompany just the first of each pair of [bass] notes [i.e., with one chord for each pair]. This is even more graceful when the [bass] notes are of short duration (that is, Quarters or Eighths); & when they are Eighths one may even accompany just the first of four [bass] notes [i.e., with one chord for every group of four]--particularly in the two-beat measure [i.e., in duple meter].

Example [121]

This [rule holds true only if] the unaccompanied [bass] notes are unfigured, as in the preceding example; for when a [bass] note is figured one must always accompany it, however short it may be--unless one clearly sees that the figure is unnecessary, & that the [bass] note can be passed over without accompaniment.[1]

You will notice furthermore that one may pass over (without specifically accompanying) just the [bass] notes that happen to occur between two beats in the measure, & not those that fall directly on the beats; for these latter ones [i.e., bass notes that fall on the beats] always need to be accompanied--except in the three-beat measure [i.e., in triple meter], as we will discuss further on.

2. When the [bass] notes progress by disjunct degrees [i.e., by leaps], one must accompany all of them (however short they may be)--except when a single chord can serve for several [bass] notes, as we have shown before in several places.

3. When the measure is in three beats [i.e., triple meter] & the Air is played quickly, one can be content with accompanying just the first [bass] note of each measure--provided that the [bass] notes move by consecutive degrees, & that the unaccompanied bass notes are unfigured (which happens very often in lively Airs [*dans les Airs guais*]).

Example [122]

p. 58

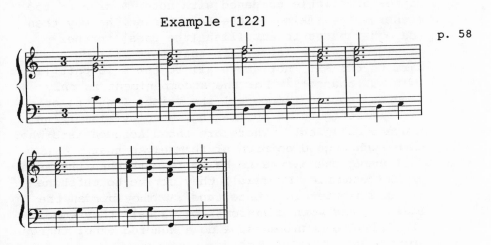

4. When the measure is so hurried [*si pressée*] that the Accompanist cannot comfortably play all of

the [bass] notes, he then can be content to play &
accompany just the first [bass] note of each mea-
sure--and thus leave it for the *Basses de Viole* or
the [*Basses de*] *Violon* to play all the [bass] notes;[2]
they can do this much more easily, since they have
no accompaniment to combine with [their bass part].
Extremely fast tempi [*les grandes vitesses*] are not
at all suited to accompanying [i.e., harmony] Instruments; this is why when the Accompanist encounters very fast passages (even in a slow measure
[i.e., meter]), he may leave them to be played by
the other Instruments; or, if he does play them, he
can reshape this fast tempo by playing only the
principal [bass] notes of these passages--that is,
the [bass] notes that fall on the principal beats of
the measure.

The principal beat of a measure (in all types of
measure [i.e., meter]) is the first beat; that one
predominates over all the others.

In the two-beat measure (of any type), the first
& second [beats] are nearly equally principal
[beats].

In the three-beat measure (either slow or fast),
the first and last [beats] are [principal beats].

And in the four-beat measure, the first & third
[beats are principal beats].

5. Contrary to what we have just said, when the
Basses are little burdened with notes & drag on too
much for the liking of the Accompanist, he may then
add other notes to embellish [the Bass] further--
provided that he is certain that this will do no
harm to the Air, nor above all to the solo part [*la
voix qui chante*].[3] For the Accompaniment is only
made to support [*seconder*] the voice, & not to sti-
fle or disfigure it by [making] a noisy clamor [*un
mauvais carillon*]. There are those Accompanists who
have such a good opinion of themselves that
(believing themselves to be worth more than the rest
of the Ensemble [*Concert*]) they strive to outshine
all of the Players [*Concertans*].[4] They burden the
Thoroughbass with divisions [*passages*]; they embellish the Accompaniments, & do a hundred other things

that perhaps are very lovely in themselves--but
which are at the time extremely detrimental to the
Ensemble, & just serve to show the vain conceit of
the Musician who produces them. Whoever plays in
Ensemble [*Concert*] ought to play for the honor & the
perfection of the Ensemble, & not for his own personal honor. It is no longer an Ensemble when
everyone plays just for himself.[5]

6. Still, the Accompanist is not obligated to
follow scrupulously the progression of the Thorough-
bass. He may descend when it ascends, or else ascend when it descends as he judges it appropriate.
That is, if [the bass] has *Ut, Sol* ascending by a
Fifth, then [the Accompanist] may play *Ut, Sol* descending by a Fourth; or, if [the bass] has [*Ut, Sol*]
descending by a Fourth, then he may play [*Ut, Sol*]
ascending by a Fifth, & so forth for all other progressions. He may even raise or lower [i.e., shift
higher or lower] the entire Bass by an Octave for
several successive measures--either to conform further to the character of the singing voice; or to
take best advantage of the [tone] quality of his
Instrument (which often resonates better in one
range of the Keyboard [*Clavier*] than in another);
or, lastly, to free up [*degager*] the hands or to
bring [them] closer together [if they happen to be]
too encumbered or too separated.   p. 59

We have said in Chapters III [pp. 20-21] & V [pp.
58-59] that the right hand should take its chords in
close position & always with contrary motion to the
Bass when the Bass moves by small intervals; nonetheless, it is permissible in some instances to
absolutely break these rules.

7. When the progression of the Bass & the contrary motion of the Accompaniment have brought the
hands together in such a way that they become en-
tangled, one can & even should at once raise [i.e.,
shift upwards] at once the right hand by leaping as
large an interval as is needed in order to free up
[the hands]; & even though this might be done with
similar motion & on a small interval in the Bass,
there is no harm done because necessity demands it.[6]

Example [123]

Instead of raising [i.e., shifting upwards] the Accompaniment in this way, one could leave out one of its parts as we have instructed previously [pp. 72-73, Rules 18 and 19]. One is free to do either-- they are both equally good.

8. When one comes upon a long [bass] note, one may move the right hand [accompaniment] farther away or closer in (depending upon whether one finds it too encumbered or too separated) by playing two chords on this single [bass] note.

Example [124]

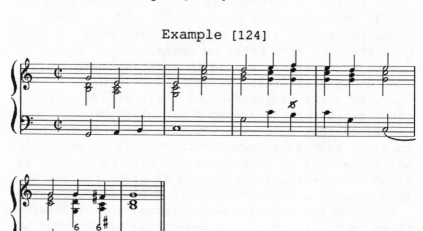

9. When a Cadence consists of just two [bass] notes, the Accompanist may substitute three [*remettre à trois*], by dividing the first [bass] note in two, & having it [i.e., the second half] sound an Octave lower; but this can be done only when the Cadence ends by descending a Fifth, & when the first [bass] note is of sufficient length to be divided.

Example [125]

10. Although consecutive Octaves and Fifths made   p. 60 with similar motion might be what is most strictly forbidden in Music, one is not too scrupulous about having them in the Accompaniment when one accompanies in a large Musical Ensemble [*Choeur*]--in which the clamor of the other Instruments covers the Harpsichord in such a way that one cannot judge whether or not it makes mistakes.[7] Besides, these mistakes (as serious as they are in Composition) ought not to count for mistakes on such occasions--because then it is merely a matter of playing the Bass accurately & making the harmony of the Parts heard, which comes about equally well when playing two Fifths or Octaves as when not playing them.[8]

But when one accompanies a single voice, one cannot adhere too religiously to correctness--above all if one is accompanying it alone [i.e., without other thoroughbass instruments]; for then everything is exposed, & the Critics will let you get away with nothing.

11. A single Part of the Accompaniment may form the Fifth against the Bass twice in succession without it being a license--provided that the first of these two Fifths is perfect, & the second [Fifth is] either false or augmented.[9]

Example [126]

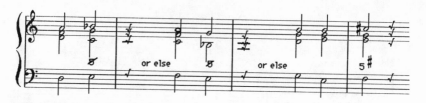

12. One Part may form first the false Fifth & then the perfect Fifth against another Part--which it cannot form against the Bass. *See* the first part of the following example [Example 127].

13. Finally, it would be only a slight license if one Part formed even the perfect Fifth against another Part twice in succession.

I know that the *greatest* regularity [i.e., adherence to the rules of accompaniment] would not allow it; but since this mistake (if it is indeed one) is not at all apparent, I maintain that one may do it boldly. For since Music is made just for the ear, a mistake that does not offend [the ear] in the least is not a mistake.[10]

Example [127] *of Fifths in the Parts*

Those are the licenses, contrary to the general principles of Accompaniment, that one may take in accompanying. The fine judgement of a skilled Accompanist perhaps might permit him still others--

of which it is not easy to speak, since they would rely solely on his good taste.   For it is known that good taste often decides things for which one can give no reason other than good taste itself; & this good taste which is so esteemed is not too clearly understood [*n'est pas trop clairement connu*] even by those who possess it.   But with regard to Accompaniment on the Harpsichord, there is a universal taste [*un gout général*] which passes for good taste--of which we will give a general idea in the following Chapter.

CHAPTER IX

ON TASTE IN ACCOMPANIMENT

[DU GOUT DE L'ACCOMPAGNEMENT]

Continuation of the choice of Chords

Just as there is a certain style & a certain good
grace to be met with in everything that men say or
do, without which the finest things are often worth
nothing, so there is also in Accompaniment with the
Harpsichord a taste & manner of accompanying which,
to the Accompaniment, is no less necessary than the
very foundation of Accompaniment itself.

1. This taste principally consists of a careful
handling of the harmony of one's Instrument--in such
a way that one does not draw so much sound [*son*]
from the Harpsichord that it entirely overwhelms the
solo voice (*la voix qui chante*), or, on the contrary, that one does not draw so little [sound] that
it does not support [the solo voice] enough. It is
necessary to conform as much as possible to the
voice one accompanies. When the singer holds back
[*quand la personne se menage*] & sings (as is said)
just in half-voice [*à demi-voix*], one must lighten
up [*soulager*] on the accompaniment--drawing less
sound from the Harpsichord by not leaning into the
keys, & even by accompanying on the small stop [*sur
le petit jeu*] if the voice is very feeble. But when
the voices are strong, as with these singers who always sing in full chest voice [*à pleine poitrine*]:
then one must pull out all the stops on the Harpsichord & strike the chords vigorously--as much as one
can without making the noise of the harpsichord's
action [*le bruit du bois*] heard; one must accompany
in the low range of the Keyboard, rather than in the
middle range; in a word, one must make as much sound
[*bruit*; i.e., volume] as the voice, but also take
care not to overpower it.[1]

2. For extremely delicate voices, one could (as
we have said) either disengage a stop or two on the
Harpsichord, or else leave out one note from each

chord--thus reducing the Accompaniment to two Parts
[i.e., two parts in addition to the bass note]; &
the Part one leaves out is that which forms the Octave against the Bass, rather than one of the other
two [Parts]--insofar as one can do this without
breaking the general rules.[2]

3. On the other hand, when the voices are stong
one may double with the left hand any of the Parts
played by the right hand; one can even double all of
them if the voices are very strong, & if [the Harp-
sichord] is not supported enough by other Instruments of the Ensemble [*Concert*]. If only one Part
is to be doubled, it should be the Octave; if two
[Parts] are to be doubled, they should be either the
Octave & Fifth, or else the Part that takes the
place of the Fifth; & if three [Parts] are to be
doubled, they should be the same [Parts] that are in
the right hand.

4. However, while filling in [Parts] in this way,
one is not obliged to include in the left hand just
the same notes that are in the right hand; on the
contrary, there is a certain elegance in choosing
other [notes]. One should include exactly the same
ones, at very most, on [bass] notes that have perfect chords [i.e., for perfect chords, one should
double just chord tones]; but as for the others
[i.e., for other than perfect chords], one should
not always handle them [i.e., the doublings] in this
manner. In the first place, one should never double
dissonances, except for the Second; thus when a
[bass] note has [a dissonance], one should fill in
by doubling just those consonances that serve as accompaniment [to the dissonance]; or, when possible,
one includes & doubles the very consonance that was
replaced by the dissonance. By way of explanation,
suppose that a [bass] note has the Seventh. The
natural Accompaniment for the Seventh is the Third &
Fifth; hence, those are the notes one should double
when one wishes to fill in. But since the Seventh   p. 62
replaces the Octave in a chord, I say that to fill
in one should include the Octave & even double it
within the Accompaniment of the Seventh. Notice,
however, that one cannot always include (in the
accompaniment of a dissonance) the consonance which
was replaced [by the dissonance], & that there are

scarcely any [dissonances] but the Seventh which may
allow it. Thus, you could fill in for the others
[i.e., dissonances other than the Seventh] by doubling just those consonances that one would usually
give for Accompaniment.[3]

5. When a [bass] note (after which the following
[bass note] ascends a tone) has a Sixth instead of a
perfect chord: then, in addition to this Sixth, one
can fill in by playing & doubling all of the notes
comprising the perfect chord.[4]

6. But in addition to filling in regularly (as we
have said in order to draw out more sound from the
Harpsichord--when it is appropriate to do so), one
also may restrike chords several times in succes-
sion--when this can be done without altering the
measure [*sans alterer la mesure*] or disfiguring the
Air. One nearly always makes use of this [techni-
que] in large Ensembles [*dans les Choeurs*].

7. It is equally good practice [*il n'est pas
moins du bon usage*] to fill in the Accompaniment
even when one accompanies just a solo voice: but
then, one does not strike all the Parts at once--
rather, one plays them one after another with discretion [*on les applique l'une aprés l'autre avec
menagement*]. This is called *to Arpeggiate* [*Harpé-
ger*] chords, & it is one of the most suitable embellishments for Accompaniment with the Harpsichord.[5]

8. Even when one does not double Parts, one still
should arpeggiate them. One could repeat a single
chord even several times, by arpeggiating it first
in ascending & then in descending. But this [arpeg-
giated] repetition must be carefully handled, and it
cannot be taught to you by a Book: rather, you must
see someone actually doing it.[6]

Arpeggios are suitable only in Recitative, where
properly speaking there is no meter [*mesure*]; for in
measured Airs [*les Airs de mouvement*], one must
strike the [right-hand] chords simultaneously with
their Bass--except when all the notes of the Bass
are Quarters & when the meter [*mesure*] is in three
beats, one may then separate the notes of each chord
in such a way that one [note] is continually held
back and sounded on the offbeats [*qu'on en reserve
toûjours une pour la faire parler entre deux temps*].

This creates a kind of pulsation [*battement*] that suits it quite well [*qui sied tout à fait bien*].[7]

Example [128]

One can also do the same thing in the two-beat measure [i.e., hold back one note of the chord to sound on the offbeats].

9. When one accompanies a long Solo [*Recit, i.e.*, a recitative], it is sometimes good to linger on a chord (when the Bass permits it) & let the voice sing several notes without accompaniment...then, to strike a second chord, & again dwell on it...& so to furnish the accompaniments [i.e., the right hand chords] intermittently [*que par de longs intervalles*]--assuming, as I have said, that the Bass has only long notes, which is quite common in Recitative [*Recitatif*].[8]

10. At other times, after having struck a filled-in chord upon which one dwells at length, one could restrike [*rebat*] a single note all by itself, here and there--but with such discretion [*menagement*] that it seems as though the Harpsichord gave them up all by itself, without the initiative of the Accompanist.

11. At other times when doubling Parts one may   p. 63 restrike all the notes one after another in a continual repetition--thereby drawing from the Harpsichord a crackling [*petillement*] a bit like a volley of musket fire; but after having made this agreeable

clamor [*agréable charivari*] for three or four mea-
sures, one then stops short on some great Harmonic
chord (that is, one without dissonance)--as if to
rest on it from the strain of making so much sound.

12. When one accompanies a solo voice that sings
a measured Air [*Air de movement*] in which there are
several melodic imitations [*imitations de chants*]
(like Italian Airs have), one could imitate on the
Harpsichord both the Subject [*Sujet*] & the Imitations [*Fugues*] of the Air--by having the Parts enter
one after another; but that [technique] requires
consummate skill [*une science comsommée*], & one must
be first rate [*du premier ordre*] to succeed at it.[9]

13. The greatest taste that one might display in
Accompaniment is to know how to adapt completely to
the character of the voices one accompanies & to
that of the Airs being sung--entering even into the
spirit of the words, & not enlivening the accompaniment when the Song speaks of Feebleness & Languor,
nor on the contrary letting it lag behind when the
Actor [i.e., the singer] becomes animated & impas-
sioned when speaking of Wrath, Vengeance, Rage, or
Fury.

Finally, since the Accompaniment exists just to
support [*seconder*] the voice, it should adapt itself
to [the voice] in every way.

14. On the Organ one does not restrike chords, &
one hardly ever uses arpeggios; on the contrary, one
ties together the pitches extensively through the
skillful fluency of the hands [*en coulant les mains
adroitement*; i.e., legato playing]. One rarely
doubles [right-hand] Parts--the Organ (which sup-
plies [part-doublings] itself much more than the
Harpsichord, & continually sustains its harmony
evenly) does not have need of all the devices one
uses with the Harpsichord in order to compensate for
the evanescence of the instrument [*pour supléer à la
secheresse de l'Instrument*].[10]

15. One may play some trills [*tremblements*] or
some other ornament from time to time--either on the
Organ or on the Harpsichord, and either in the Bass
or in the Parts--should one decide that the passages
require it. One always plays a $\overset{3}{\text{trill}}$ on a [bass]
note that has a doubled chord [$\overset{6}{\underset{3}{}}$ or $\overset{3}{\underset{6}{}}$] when this
note is of ample value. One also plays [a trill]

on the penultimate [bass note] of imperfect Caden-
ces--the [type] that end by successive degrees
[i.e., semitones and tones], & not by intervals
[i.e., leaps].[11]

Example [129]

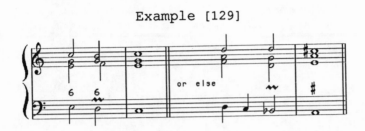

For these two types of Cadences, instead of playing the trill on the Bass note where it is indicated
here one could play it on the note in the Accompaniment that forms the Sixth against this Bass [note]:
but sometimes the position of the [right] hand does
not permit [one to play a trill there], & besides,
[the trill] is more graceful in the Bass than in the
Parts. One could play [a trill] in the Bass & in
the Parts simultaneously; but I would not wish it
done for every one of these types of Cadences--that
would be too affected.

16. In order to tie chords together [*pour lier
les accords entr'eux*] & to make them appear not so
disjointed [*si plaquez*], one may play on some occasions the note found in the melodic line [*chemin*] of
a Part that is moving by the interval of a Third
[i.e., on the passing note]--in the manner that I
have shown in the first Example of page 39 [Example
57], & perhaps elsewhere.

Just as one is not obliged to play three differ-   p. 64
ent Parts in a chord of the [right-hand] accompaniment at all times (since one is free to double some
of [the Parts] when one wishes to, or even to leave
out one of the three [Parts] when that seems necessary), one can also sometimes provide a fourth
[Part] in the chords assigned by the general Rules--
either to soften the harshness of a dissonance, or,
on the contrary, to make it more piquant so as to
better savor its resolution to a consonance. To say
which interval this fourth note should form against

the Bass would require too detailed an explanation;
it would be necessary to re-examine individually all
of the Tonalities & all of the chords. Let your ear
be the judge of it when the occasion presents itself; & if you cannot decide, then leave it out.

CONCLUSION

I could add here a Recapitulation like the one I
included at the end of the *Principles of the Harpsichord*, but that does not seem very necessary. Those
who start Accompanying are not novices in Musical
matters. They know that: [1] before accompanying an
Air one should observe in which Tonality & Mode it
is composed, in order to play [i.e., to improvise] a
short Prelude in that particular Tonality; [2] one
should examine the meter [*mesure*] & the tempo
[*mouvement*]; [3] in the course of the Air one must
see whether the Mode, the Meter [*Mesure*], or the
Clef might change; [4] one should take heed of the
Figures pertaining to the [bass] notes, as well as
of the Sharps and Flats that might be attached to
these Figures; [5] one should take into account the
progression of the Bass, in order to provide Figures
wherever they might be lacking; [6] in a word, one
should put into practice all of the rules [*précep-
tes*] that one has acquired. When one begins to
learn Pieces [i.e., solo harpsichord compositions],
one is not yet familiar with all the symbols of
Notation & the observations they require; but when
one starts to accompany, one usually knows all of
that by heart & does not need to be warned to take
heed of them.

E N D

N O T E S

PREFACE

1. *Les Principes du Clavecin, contenant une Explication exacte de tout ce qui concerne la Tablature & le Clavier* (Paris: Christophe Ballard, 1702); trans. and ed. by Rebecca Harris-Warrick, *Principles of the Harpsichord by Monsieur de Saint Lambert* (Cambridge University Press, 1984).

2. Other accompaniment treatises with which Saint Lambert might have been familiar are: Jean-Henri d'Anglebert's *Principes de L'Accompagnement* (contained in *Pièces de clavecin* [Paris: Chez l'auteur, 1689]; facsimile repr., New York: Broude Brothers, 1965), Guillaume-Gabriel Nivers's *L'Art d'accompagner sur la basse-continue pour l'orgue et le clavecin* (Paris: l'Auteur, 1689), Denis Delair's *Traité d'acompagnement pour le théorbe, et le clavessin* (Paris: Chez l'auteur, 1690; facsimile reprint, Geneva: Minkoff, 1972), and Jacques Boyvin's *Traité abrégé de l'accompagnement pour l'orgue et pour le clavecin* (Paris: Christophe Ballard, 1700).

3. Here, Saint Lambert acknowledges that a student of accompaniment may or may not be acquainted with the fundamentals of music notation or keyboard technique before he begins the study of the thoroughbass; however, in his Conclusion (p. 115) Saint Lambert says that he assumes the student has undertaken a thorough study of musical notation *before* attempting to learn accompaniment.

Most other writers of the eighteenth century recommend that students first attain a certain amount of keyboard facility. Couperin (*L'art de toucher le clavecin* [Paris, 1717]) writes:

> Je finis ce discours par donner un conseil à
> ceux qui veulent rèüssir parfaitement dans les
> pièces! C'est d'estre deux ou trois ans avant que
> d'aprendre L'accompagnement. Les raisons que j'en
> donne sont fondées. 1°. Les basses-continuës qui
> ont un progrès chantant, devant être èxècutées de
> la main gauche avec autant de propreté que les

Pièces, jl est nècèssaire d'en sçavoir fort bien
joüer. 2°. La main droite dans L'accompagnement
n'ètant occupée qu'à faire des accords, est tou-
jours dans une extension capable de la rendre tres
roide; ainsi les pièces qu'on aura aprises
d'abord, serviront à prèvenir cet inconvènient.
Enfin la vivacité avec laquelle on se porte à exe-
cuter la musique à L'ouverture du Livre entraînant
avec soi une façon de toucher ferme, et souvent
pesante, le jeu courerisque de s'en ressentir, à
moins qu'on n'exerce les pièces alternativement
avec L'accompagnement.

[I end this discourse by giving advice to those
who wish to succeed perfectly with the pieces: it
is to wait two or three years before learning accompaniment. The reasons that I give for this are
well-founded. 1st, since the thoroughbasses [bass
lines] with a melodic progression need to be
played by the left hand with as much precision as
the pieces, it is necessary to know how to play
them very well. 2nd, since the right hand in the
accompaniment is occupied only with playing
chords, it is always extended in such a way that
is capable of rendering it very stiff; thus the
pieces that one learns first will serve to prevent
this ill-consequence. Finally, the rapidity with
which one is inclined to play the music at the beginning of the Book entails with it a fashion of
playing firmly and often heavily--the effects of
which will run the risk of being felt unless one
were to practice the pieces and the accompaniment
alternatively.]

4. Here Saint Lambert suggests that the 1707 edition of the *Nouveau traité* is the first edition and
not, as Fétis (*Biographie universelle VII*, 371-72)
and later F. T. Arnold (*The Art of Accompaniment
from a Thoroughbass* [London, 1931], 172-73) claim, a
second edition of a treatise dating from 1680. See
Introduction, p. xi.
5. Saint Lambert is referring to the seventeenth-
century custom of using Dorian key-signatures for
the minor keys, which had one flat less than the
modern minor key-signature. The untransposed Dorian
mode, with its occasional use of Bb, was adopted as

the prototype for minor by seventeenth-century French theorists; Delair, for instance, uses modern minor key-signatures for sharp keys, but his minor flat keys all bear Dorian signatures. Saint Lambert was the first in France to use A-minor as the model for all minor keys. English theorists, on the other hand, used the Aeolian mode (with B*b* in the signature) for minor keys.

See Imogene Horsley's introduction to Masson's *Nouveau traité des règles de la composition de la musique par lequel on apprend à faire facilement un chant sur des paroles* (Paris, 1694; repr. New York: Da Capo Press, 1967), pp. vii-ix, for a more complete discussion of this topic.

6. Although Nivers also was the author of a treatise on accompaniment (*L'Art d'accompagner*), Saint Lambert no doubt refers here to Nivers's treatise on composition, *Traité de la composition de musique* (Paris: L'Auteur et Robert Ballard, 1667); trans. and ed. by Albert Cohen (*Treatise on the Composition of Music* [New York: Institute of Mediaeval Music, 1965]). Masson's composition treatise is cited above in n. 2.

7. Sebastien de Brossard, *Dictionnaire de musique, contenant une explication des termes grecs, latins, italiens, et françois les plus usitez dans la musique* (Paris: Christophe Ballard, 1703); trans. and ed. by Albion Gruber (Sebastien de Brossard: *Dictionary of Music* [Henryville: Institute of Mediaeval Music, Ltd., 1982]).

8. Etienne Loulié (*Elements ou principes de musique* [Paris: Christophe Ballard, 1696]; trans. and ed. by Albert Cohen, *Etienne Loulié: Elements or Principles of Music* [New York: Institute of Mediaeval Music, 1965], pp. 48-49) distinguishes between *accidental* and *essential* sharps and flats:

> Dependent Sounds are the sharpened or flattened Principal Sounds. An Accidental Sharp or Flat characterizes a Dependent Sound; it occurs during the course of a melody. An Essential Sharp or Flat is one indicated immediately after the clef ([it is also known as a] sharp or flat of the clef).

9. Therefore, rewording Saint Lambert's statement using Loulié's terminology: in minor flat tonalities the flatted Sixth is one of the principal sounds (rather than one of the dependent sounds), and as a principal sound it should be indicated by an essential flat in the key-signature (and not as an accidental flat in the course of the melody).

10. Saint Lambert discusses the three chord arrangements on pp. 20-21; they are distinguished by the Third, the Fifth, or the Octave being the highest part.

11. Saint Lambert's use of the term *Modulation* here and elsewhere does not precisely correspond to the modern meaning of the term. Brossard (*Dictionnaire de musique*, trans. Gruber) defines the term as follows:

> ...To modulate, according to the moderns, is not only to have a melody proceed by the essential and natural notes of the mode more often than by others, but also to use these same notes in the harmony parts more often and in preference to others that should be avoided. Not that these last are not good, but that they would often go out of the mode inappropriately.
>
> To modulate is also to go out of the mode at times, but only in order to return appropriately and naturally. Further, it is to give to melody a variety of movement and of different figures which render it expressive without being dull or too affected. Lastly, it is to give to the composition that certain elusive charm and graciousness which long and frequent practice might sometimes produce, which a happy talent provides often naturally and effortlessly, and which is called *beauchant*.

As Masson (*Nouveau traité des règles pour la composition*, p. 9; see also Ch. 4, n. 4) explains, the essential notes for each major and minor tonality are the tonic (*finale*), the mediant (*médiante*), and the dominant (*dominante*). Saint Lambert's term *modulation* therefore best fits the first part of Brossard's definition. By "forcing the Modulation" Saint Lambert presumably means introducing notes

other than the essential and natural notes in such a
way that the melodic and harmonic progression is
awkward and goes out of the mode inappropriately.

CHAPTER 1

1. *Thoroughbass* has been used in this edition as
an eighteenth-century English term equivalent to the
French term *basse-continuë*.

2. Jean-Jacques Rousseau, who contributed ar-
ticles on music for Diderot's *Encyclopédie* (Paris:
Briasson, David, Le Breton, & Durand, 1751-65; repr.
New York: Pergamon Press, 1985) explains that "*Harmony*, according to the moderns, is, properly speaking, the effect of several pitches heard at once
when it results in a pleasant ensemble--in this
sense harmony and chord means the same thing. But
this word more commonly is used to mean an orderly
succession of several chords" (*Encyclopédie*, s.v.
Harmonie).

Saint Lambert later uses the terms *son*, *corde*,
and *note*, with slight differences in meaning, to refer to musical pitch. According to the *Encyclopédie*, *son* is "a type of sound [*bruit*]" which has the
properties of degree of elevation, dynamic level,
and quality of timbre. *Corde* refers to both the
string of the instrument, as well as the *son* created
by it. Both *son* and *corde*, when used to refer to
musical pitch, will be henceforth translated simply
as "pitch."

Saint Lambert also uses the term *note* to distinguish the seven pitches used in solmization, as well
as to refer to the written symbol for a note. This
term will be translated as "note."

3. Jean-Philippe Rameau (*Traité de l'harmonie réduite à ses principes naturels*, Book IV [Paris: Ballard, 1722]) borrowed this passage from Saint Lambert with few changes:

Saint Lambert, p. 2	Rameau, p. 363
Le Clavecin contenant tous les sons qui peuvent entrer dans la construction des ouvrages de Musique, il est aisé d'en remarquer la difference, en touchant toutes les touches l'une aprés l'autre; car si l'on commence à gauche, & que l'on tire vers la	Le Clavecin ou l'Orgue contenant tous les Sons qui peuvent entrer dans la Composition des Ouvrages de Musique, il est aisé d'en remarquer la difference, en touchant chaque Touche l'une après l'autre; car si l'on commence à gauche en tirant à droite,

droite, on trouvera que les sons
vont toûjours en s'élevant, c'est
-à-dire en s'éclaircissant: & si
l'on commence à droit, & que l'on
tire vers la gauche, on trouvera
qu'il vont en baissant, c'est-à-dire
en grossissant.

l'on trouvera que les Sons vont
toûjours en s'élevant; & si l'on
commence à droite en tirant à
gauche, l'on trouvera qu'ils vont
en baissant.

The *Encyclopédie* (s.v. *Touche*) explains that the
term has various meanings: for guitars, lutes,
theorboes, and similar instruments, *touche* can refer
either to the fingerboard of the instrument or to
the strings. For organs, spinets, and harpsichords,
touche refers to the ebony or ivory keys of the keyboard.

4. In *Les Principes du clavecin*, p. 36 and pp.
62-64, Saint Lambert explains that the accidentals
encountered most often are C#, F#, G#, Bb, and Eb;
his illustration of the keyboard (p. 6) names accidentals in this way.

5. That is to say, the white (ivory) sharps and
flats along with the black (ebony) natural keys.
During Saint Lambert's time, the color-scheme of the
keys on French harpsichords was the reverse of the
modern piano keyboard; for an illustration, see *Les
Principes du clavecin*, p. 6 (repr. in Harris-Warrick, p. 18). Here (p. 7), Saint Lambert mentions
that "some people call the white keys in general
"accidentals" [*feintes*]," but in Chapter 14 (p. 35)
he explains that "Accidentals are the symbols in
Tablature [i.e., notation] created in order to
change the natural Pitch of particular Notes to
another Pitch. There are three types of Accidentals: the Sharp, the Flat, and the Natural."

6. Saint Lambert later distinguishes between
these two kinds of semitones (minor and major) in
Rule 17, p. 70.

7. Discussed in Chapter 2.

8. By *Tablature* Saint Lambert refers to notation
in general rather than to music tablature in which,
according to Brossard (*Dictionnaire de musique*,
trans. Gruber; s.v. *Tablatura*), "alphabet letters,
numbers, or some other signs not common to modern
music are used to represent the notes." This is
borne out by the title of Saint Lambert's treatise
of 1702 (*Les Principes du Clavecin, contenant une
Explication exacte de toute ce qui concerne la Tablature & le Clavier*), wherein the author describes
standard notation rather than keyboard tablature.

Loulié (*Elements ou principes de musique*, trans. Cohen, p. 11) defines the term *degré* as a line or a space on the musical staff; the *Encyclopédie* further defines *degré* as the difference in position or elevation between two notes placed on the same staff. Therefore, Saint Lambert's use of the terms *son* to designate pitch and *degré* to designate position suggests the following paraphrase of the last sentence: "And it is for the same reason that in Musical Notation the seven pitches [that is, *ut, re, mi, fa, sol, la,* and *si*] have specific lines and spaces assigned to them on the staff, while the sharps and flats do not."

9. Rameau (*Traité de l'harmonie*, Book IV) also borrowed this paragraph from Saint Lambert with slight modification:

<table>
<tr><td>Saint Lambert, pp. 2-3</td><td>Rameau, p. 364</td></tr>
<tr><td>

Les sept sons, *ut, re, mi, fa, sol, la, si,* étant d'un usage incomparablement plus frequent que les autres, sont considerez comme s'ils étoient les seuls qui entrassent dans la composition des piéces. Ainsi dans la suite de ce Traité, nous établirons toûjours nos régles par rapport à ces sept sons, & nous les appellerons les sept notes de la Musique, parce qu'ils sont ordinairement connus sous ce nom & sous cette idée.

</td><td>

Les sept Nottes *Ut, Ré, Mi, Fa, Sol, La, Si,* étant d'un usage incomparablement plus frequent que les autres sont considerées dans la Musique commes les seules qui entrent dans la Composition; c'est pourquoi nous établirons toûjours nos Regles sur ces sept Nottes, qui doivent se prendre sur les Touches naturelles du Clavier; & il ne faut faire attention aux *Diezes* ni aux *B-mols* qui separent ces Touches, que lorsqu'il sont absolument necessaires pour former l'Intervalle que l'on s'est proposé.

</td></tr>
</table>

10. Refer to note 8 above for Loulié's definition of the term *degré*.

11. Interval names will be capitalized from here on in order to avoid confusion.

CHAPTER 2

1. Jean-Philippe Rameau (*Traité de l'harmonie*, Book IV) borrows this passage with few changes:

<table>
<tr><td>Saint Lambert, p. 5</td><td>Rameau, p. 368</td></tr>
<tr><td>

La nature & les diverses especes de chaque intervalle étant expliquees, comme nous venons de le faire, il faut que celui qui veut sçavoir l'Accompagnement s'applique à trouver de soi-même sur le Clavier tous les intervalles de chaque note ou touche, & toutes leurs diverses especes; & il faut qu'il se rendre cette connoissance si familiere, que quelque touche qu'on lui montre, il puisse dire

</td><td>

La nature & les diverses especes de chaque Intervale étant expliquées, il faut que celui qui veut sçavoir l'Accompagnement, s'applique à trouver de lui-même sur le Clavier tous differens Intervales de chaque Notte, ou Touche, & toutes leurs diverses especes, en se rendant cette connoissance si familiere, que quelque Notte ou Touche qu'il s'imagine, il

</td></tr>
</table>

tout d'un coup quelle autre touche
en est la tierce majeure, ou la mineure, ou la quatre, ou le Triton, ou
la septiéme, &c.

puisse dire & toucher tout d'un
coup celle qui en est la Tierce
mineure ou majeure, la Sixte, le
Tri-Ton, la Quinte juste, diminuée ou superfluë, la Septiéme,
&c.

2. Saint Lambert never does return to this topic.
The intervals that he labels *rare* in the following
example for the most part use enharmonic spellings
of natural notes (i.e., C-flat, E-sharp, F-flat, and
B-sharp).

3. Apparently, this work was never accomplished.

4. See pp. 36-37.

5. Brossard (*Dictionnaire de musique*, s.v. *Inter-
vallo*) also uses the terms simple, double, triple,
and quadruple in discussing compound intervals, and
he recommends subtracting multiples of seven in order to reduce compound intervals to their simple
forms.

6. See below, p. 32 and pp. 35-37. Masson (*Nouveau traité des règles pour la composition*, p. 60)
explains that:

> On distingue la neuviéme de la seconde dans la
> Composition, en ce que la neuviéme se trouve
> toûjours sur la première partie d'une note ronde
> d'une Basse, ou sur la première de deux notes
> blanches en même degré, de deux noires ou de deux
> croches; & que la seconde ne se trouve que sur la
> derniére partie de la note ronde de la Basse, ou
> sur la seconde des deux blanches en même degré,
> des deux noires, ou des deux croches, & de plus en
> ce qu'elles exigent des accompagnemens differens,
> comme il en sera parlé dans la Composition à
> quatre Parties.

> [One distinguishes the Ninth from the Second in
> Composition insofar as the Ninth is always found
> either on the first part of a whole-note in the
> Bass, or on the first of two half-notes on the
> same degree (or on two quarter-notes, or on two
> eighth-notes); & the Second is just found either
> on the last part of the whole-note in the Bass, or
> on the second of two half-notes on the same degree
> (or on two quarter-notes, or on two eighth-notes);
> & moreover insofar as they require different ac-
> companiments, as will be discussed in "Composition
> in four Parts."]

According to Nicolas Bernier's rare manuscript *Principes de composition* (before 1734; trans. George Schuetze Jr. [New York: Institute of Mediaeval Music, 1964]), the Ninth may be used only in three cases: (1) when the bass ascends one degree from the weak beat to the strong beat, (2) when it makes a skip of a Fourth in ascending, and (3) when it makes a skip of a Fifth in descending from the weak beat to the strong beat.

CHAPTER 3

1. Saint Lambert gives most of his examples in four-part harmony, the bass played with the left hand and the three parts (the accompaniment) played with the right. Later, Saint Lambert discusses circumstances (such as avoiding consecutive perfect intervals or improper progressions [pp. 72-73], or accomodating weak voices [pp. 108-109]) for which the accompanist may decide to reduce the harmony to three parts. In his final Chapter (pp. 109-10) he discusses techniques of filling out the harmony by doubling chord tones in the left hand and including chord tones in addition to those called for by the figures.

Nivers's *L'Art d'accompagner* states that in four-voice accompaniment each hand should have two parts, although at times three parts can be played by the right hand (see William Pruitt, "The Organ Works of G. G. Nivers [1632-1714]," *Recherches sur la Musique française classique*, 14 [1974], p. 41); here Nivers primarily describes organ accompaniment, in which a more legato style is facilitated by dividing the four parts between the hands--and filling-in chord tones with the left hand would be avoided (cf. *Nouveau traité*, p. 112). D'Anglebert's *Principes de L'Accompagnement* (p. 125) advises: "One can fill in with the two hands on the harpsichord when the tempo is slow, but not on the organ where only four parts are necessary." Delair's *Traité d'acompagnement* (p. 57) describes more fully the type of accompaniment that is best suited to the harpsichord:

Il y a plusieurs manieres d'acompagner sur le
Clavessin, les uns ne sonnent que la basse de la
main gauche, faisant les acompagnemens de la main
droite, les autres font des acords de la main gauche aussi bien que de la droite; mais pour décider
entre ces deux manieres, je diray qu'elle[s] sont
toutes deux bonnes, pourvû qu'on ne se serve de la
premiere maniere que dans les basses de mouuement
leger se servant de la second maniere, dans les
pieces ou le mouuement est lent.

[There are several manners of accompanying on
the Harpsichord: some play the bass just with the
left hand, while forming the accompaniments with
the right hand; others form the chords with the
left hand as well as with the right; but in order
to decide between these two manners, I will say
that they are both good--provided that one employs
the first manner mainly for basses in quick tempo,
and the second manner for pieces in which the
tempo is slow.]

2. The *Encyclopédie* (s.v. *Air*) defines the term
as follows:

An *Air* in Music is, properly speaking, the melody
[*chant*] that one adapts to the words of either a
chanson [i.e., a short, informal poem] or a short
piece of Poetry that is suitable for singing; &
consequently, one calls the chanson itself an *air*.
In Opera, one applies the term *air* to all pieces
of measured music--to distinguish them from
recitative which is not [measured]; & generally,
one calls any piece of music (either vocal or instrumental) that has a beginning and end an *air*.
If the theme [*sujet*] is divided among two parts,
the air is called a *duo*; if among three, a *trio*;
etc.

3. Here Saint Lambert uses the figure 2 to signi-
fy signify $\frac{5}{4}$; later (p. 43) he offers the possibility
of interpreting it as $\frac{6}{4}$ ("When the [bass] note has
just Two [&] Four $\frac{4}{2}$, or 2 alone, one could still give
it the minor chord of its Second. . ."). Nivers
(*Traité de la composition*), Delair (*Traité d'acompagnement*), Masson (*Nouveau traité des règles pour*

la composition), and Boyvin (*Traité abrégé de l'accompagnement*) also recommend that a 2 be accompanied
by either a 5, $\overset{5}{4}$, or $\overset{6}{4}$, although later theorists (including Couperin, Corrette, Dubugrarre, La Porte,
Roussier, Heinichen, and Mattheson accompany 2 with
$\overset{6}{4}$--and require that $\overset{5}{2}$ or $\overset{5}{\underset{2}{4}}$ be figured as such.

Delair (p. 25) further suggests that it is old-
fashioned to combine the Fifth with a Second, and
that the Fifth should be used with the Second only
under special conditions:

> Il faut remarquer que les anciens metoient, or-
> dinairement la quinte, avec la seconde, au lieu de
> la sexte, comme l'on peut voir dans les oeuures de
> du Cauroy, et d'autres habiles compositeurs, néan-
> moins dans les coeurs d'opera, on y rencontre tou-
> jours la sexte, il est vray que sur les notes ou
> l'on fait la tierce mineure deuant la second, la
> sexte est vn acompagnement plus harmonieux, à la
> seconde que la quinte, mais sur les notes ou la
> tierce majeure précede la second, la quinte y est
> vn acompagnement plus harmonieux que la sexte,
> ainsi quand on acompagne qu'vne, deux, ou trois
> voix, on peut acompagner la seconde de la quinte,
> principalement lors que la tierce majeure la pré-
> cede, et lors que l'on acompagne quelque coeur de
> musique, on y mettra la sexte ou l'on doublera la
> seconde, ou la quarte, au lieu de la sexte.

> [It must be pointed out that our forebears
> usually would combine the Fifth (instead of the
> Sixth) with the Second--as can be seen in the
> works of Du Caurroy and other skilled composers;
> nevertheless, in operatic choral/orchestral num-
> bers, one always encounters the Sixth; it is true
> that, on bass notes for which one plays the minor
> Third before the Second, the Sixth is a more har-
> monious accompaniment when joined with the Second
> than with the Fifth; but on bass notes where the
> major Third precedes the Second, the Fifth is a
> more harmonious accompaniment than is the Sixth.
> Thus when one accompanies just one, two, or three
> voices, one may accompany the Second with the
> Fifth--particularly when the major Third precedes
> it. And when accompanying a choral/orchestral
> piece, one will combine the Sixth [with the Sec-

ond]--where one will double either the Second or
the Fourth instead of the Sixth.]

4. Here Saint Lambert states that for a perfect
chord figured 3, 3#, or 3b, only the bass note
[i.e., the root of the chord] is doubled in the
right hand realization.

5. Delair (*Traité d'acompagnement*), Masson (*Nouveau traité des règles pour la composition*), and
Nivers (*Traité de la composition*) allow the 4 to be
accompanied by either 5 or 6; Delair and Masson also
allow 4 to be interpreted as $\frac{6}{4}$.

6. Saint Lambert's example shows that the Bass
note following the $\frac{6}{4}$ chord must also bear a Sixth.

7. Saint Lambert therefore uses the figure #4 to
signify not only #$\frac{6}{2}$ (its traditional meaning), but
also $\frac{8}{6}$ and #$\frac{6}{2}$. Later (p. 43), he apparently contra-
dicts himself in stating: "When the [bass] note has
just Two & Tritone $2^{4\#}$, or else Tritone & Six $4\#^6$, or
else the Tritone alone 4#, its accompaniment would
always be the major chord of its Second [i.e., #$\frac{6}{4}$]."

According to Saint Lambert, there are three instances for which the bass movement determines the
accompaniment of the 4#: for a (1) #$\frac{6}{2}$ or a $\frac{6}{8\#4}$, when
the bass afterwards descends a tone, (2) $\frac{6}{\#4}$, when
the bass afterwards descends a Fourth to a perfect
chord, and (3) #$\frac{6}{3}$, when the bass descends a semitone
to a perfect chord. In the first instance, Delair
(*Traité d'acompagnement*) and Boyvin (*Traité abrégé
de l'accompagnement*) permit only #$\frac{6}{2}$; in the second
instance, Delair, Boyvin, and Masson (*Nouveau traité des règles pour la composition*) are in agreement;
and in the third instance, Delair also allows #$\frac{6}{3}$.

8. Delair (*Traité d'acompagnement*), Masson (*Nouveau traité des règles pour la composition*), and
Boyvin (*Traité abrégé de l'accompagnement*) recommend
the same accompaniment for the false Fifth; Delair
also allows the accompaniment of the diminished
Seventh and Third.

9. Masson (*Nouveau traité des règles pour la com-
position*) allows #$\frac{7}{8}$, #$\frac{9}{3}$, or $\frac{9}{\#5}$; Heinichen and Mattheson
allow only #$\frac{9}{5}$.

The #$\frac{9}{3}$ and $\frac{9}{\#5}$ chords are particularly characteris-
tic of French music of this time. Bernier (*Princi-*

pes de composition) says that the augmented Fifth
should be accompanied with the Third, but one accompanies it most often with the Ninth; also, the augmented Fifth is used when one can regularly form the
Ninth on the same note. Elsewhere, Bernier explains
that the augmented Fifth serves to embellish the
Ninth; see below, n. 14.

10. Delair (*Traité d'acompagnement*) accompanies
a bass note raised by a sharp and figured with a 6
with the chord $\frac{6}{3}$. When the note is not raised, he
accompanies it with $\frac{6}{3}$ $\frac{8}{}$, and when the bass note descends a tone to a perfect chord, he accompanies it
with $\frac{6}{4}$ $\flat 3$--assuming that the Sixth is major and the
Fourth is prepared.

11. These various forms of the chord of the Sixth
(i.e., the simple chord $\frac{6}{3}$ $\frac{8}{}$, the doubled chord $\frac{6}{3}$ or $\frac{6}{3}$,
and the little chord $\frac{6}{4}$ $\flat 3$) were all represented by the
figure "6". French theorists had a particular
liking for the little chord $\frac{6}{4}$ 3; it is also described
by Delair (*Traité d'acompagnement*, p. 28), by François Campion (*Traité d'accompagnement et de composition selon la règle des octaves de musique*, 1716,
p. 11), and by J. F. Dandrieu (*Principes de l'acompagnement du clavecin*, 1718, p. 18).

12. Saint Lambert is in general agreement with
Boyvin (*Traité abrégé de l'accompagnement*), pp. 11-
13) and Masson (*Nouveau traité des règles pour la
composition*), who accompany a bass note figured 7
with the chord $\frac{7}{5}$ $\frac{8}{3}$, or sometimes $\frac{7}{5}$ 3 to avoid parallel
Octaves or Fifths; Delair makes the distinction be-
tween the accompaniment of a 7 that resolves on a
stationary bass note, and that of a 7 that resolves
on a new bass note--although he permits the chord $\frac{7}{5}$ 3
in both instances. Later, Bernier (*Principes de
composition*) will suggest combining the Seventh with
the Third or the Ninth in three-part composition,
while in four- and five-part writing one can also
use the Fifth or Octave.

13. In ex. 20 however, the fourth measure shows a
Seventh (following a major chord with the Third on
top) accompanied with the Octave and Third, rather
than with the doubled Third.

14. In many later examples Saint Lambert does not
always follow his own rules: see exx. 14, 30, 32,
33, and 34. Later (p. 43) Saint Lambert also men-

tions the $\substack{9\\7\\5}$ chord in which both the Fifth and Seventh (but not the Third) are included in the accompaniment of the Ninth.

Other theorists apparently did not distinguish between the major Ninth (accompanied $\substack{9\\5\\3}$), and the minor Ninth (accompanied $\substack{9\\7\\3}$). The chord $\substack{9\\5\\3}$ is the accompaniment most often recommended for the figure 9; Delair includes the Seventh and Fourth, and Masson includes the Seventh and augmented Fifth, as other possibilities.

Bernier (*Principes de composition, passim.*) says that the Ninth is prepared by the Third or Fifth, and should resolve to the interval of the Third, Sixth, or Octave by descending one degree: "it is also used with the Third, Fifth, or augmented Fifth, and sometimes with the Seventh—these three intervals serving to embellish it. . .In three-part writing, the Ninth is used with the Third, Fourth, or Seventh [i.e., $\substack{9\\3}$, $\substack{9\\4}$, or $\substack{9\\7}$]; in four-part writing, the Fifth or augmented Fifth is added [$\substack{9\\5\\3}$ and $\substack{9\\\#5\\3}$; Bernier's examples also show $\substack{9\\7\\3}$, $\substack{9\\b5\\3}$, and $\substack{9\\4\\3}$]; and in five-part writing, the Seventh is added or the Third or Fifth is doubled [$\substack{9\\7\\5}$ or $\substack{9\\7\\\#5}$]. . .When the Fourth and Ninth are used at the same time, they may be accompanied with the Third in a lower part [$\substack{9\\4\\3}$; Bernier's example also shows $\substack{9\\b5\\4}$]."

15. Cf. p. 43, paragraphs 3 and 4; later, it became more common to combine $\substack{4\\2}$ with the Sixth.

16. Saint Lambert here distinguishes between the simple chord of the Sixth $\substack{8\\6\\3}$, figured $\substack{6\\3}$, and the chord of the double Sixth $\substack{6\\3\\6}$ or the double Third $\substack{6\\3}$, both figured 6.

17. In his examples, Saint Lambert breaks this rule as frequently as he follows it.

18. The $\substack{6\\\#4}$ chord rarely is discussed in the treatises of Saint Lambert's contemporaries.

19. Other theorists do not distinguish between the different accompaniments given to $\substack{b7\\4}$, as Saint Lambert does; most recommend either $\substack{b7\\5\\4}$ or $\substack{8\\b7\\4}$.

20. Cf. p. 43 above, last paragraph. Other theorists of this time recommend the $\substack{9\\5\\4}$ chord.

21. Marc-Antoine Charpentier, *Medée* (Paris: Christophe Ballard, 1693); on p. 8, Charpentier figures $\substack{11\\9}$ resolving to $\substack{10\\8}$, instead of $\substack{9\\4}$ resolving to $\substack{8\\3}$.

22. The figure $^{10}_8$ also appears on pp. 93 and 95.

23. In other words, when representing compound intervals it is better to substitute basic figures. A literal translation of this convoluted sentence is: "Any interval that is but the repetition of another does not need to be figured precisely as it is: it is better instead to figure the one of which it is the repetition."

24. Here, Saint Lambert refers to the approach toward a bass note figured 9: if the bass ascends to form a 9 with a (stationary) part of the accompaniment, it is then treated as a Ninth (and the upper part resolves downward, as in ex. 23); if on the other hand the bass remains on the same scale degree for the figured note or if it descends a tone, the Ninth is then treated as a Second (and the bass resolves downward, as in exx. 4-6). Ex. 34 (m. 4) is not covered by these rules, whereby a Ninth is formed on a bass note approached by a descending Fifth.

25. See Chapter 3, notes 9 and 14 above. Delair (*Traité d'acompagnement*) furnishes a bass note figured $\#^7_5$ with a $\#^9_5$ chord.

26. Saint Lambert's $^3_7$ agrees with other contemporary theorists, who often suggest $^9_7$ as well. On pp. 43-44, however, Saint Lambert is not in agreement with theorists when he states that the accompaniment of a $^9_7$ may be the perfect chord of the note a tone lower, or $^9_7$; cf. Ch. 3, n. 14 above.

27. The logic of this rule becomes clear if one considers that the Ninth and the Seventh are suspensions, which are (presumably) prepared in the previous right-hand chord. See also Rule 20, p. 74.

28. According to the *Encyclopédie* (s.v. *Chant*), this term refers specifically to vocal music as well as more generally to "the manner of conducting the melody in all types of airs and pieces of music." Saint Lambert has in mind primarily a vocal soloist, and secondarily an instrumentalist, when he uses the terms *chant* and *partie chantante* (see pp. 56-57, where he refers to the soloist as *une voix*); these terms have been translated here as "melodic line" and "solo part."

29. "Par l'*Ut*, & par le *Ré*," i.e., on bass progressions for which the final is *Ut* and *Re*. Saint

Lambert postpones speaking in terms of tonality until the beginning of Chapter 4.

30. Saint Lambert's method for relating compound figures to perfect chords superimposed at some interval above a bass note appears to derive from Delair's treatise (*Traité d'acompagnement*, pp. 30-31). Delair relates compound figures to the perfect chord (*l'acord naturel*), the chord of the Ninth, and the chord of the false Fifth (he is unable to relate the $\frac{5}{4}$ chord to these three chords). Michel Corrette (*Le Maître de clavecin pour l'accompagnement, methode theorique et pratique*, 1753, pp. 34ff) draws upon the system of Delair and Saint Lambert--referring to it as finding chords "by supposition."

31. See p. 33, where he prefers the realization $\begin{smallmatrix}5\\4\\2\end{smallmatrix}$.

32. See p. 35, where he combines $\sharp\overset{6}{4}$ with the Octave.

33. Whereas Saint Lambert here interprets $\overset{9}{7}$ as the perfect chord of a tone lower than the bass note (i.e., as a $\overset{9}{\underset{4}{7}}$), Delair relates it to the chord of the false Fifth (i.e., as a $\overset{9}{\underset{5}{7}}$). See also Ch. 3, n. 14.

34. See *Les Principes du Clavecin*, Ch. 8, p. 14.

35. Saint Lambert's definition of perfect cadence then requires the bass to ascend a Fourth or to descend a Fifth; it should be noted that, unlike earlier theorists (e.g. Masson *Nouveau traité des règles pour la composition*, p. 50), Saint Lambert does not specifically require the outer voices to cadence at the Octave--although his example of the perfect cadence (ex. 39) in fact does so.

36. Although Saint Lambert's description of the interrupted cadence is ambiguous, Ex. 40 clearly shows the bass line ascending a Second rather than a Fourth (thereby forming a V^7-vi cadence).

The *Encyclopédie* (s.v. *Cadence*), following Rameau's definition, describes the *cadence rompue* as one "in which the fundamental bass, instead of ascending a Fourth after a Seventh-chord, as in the *cadence parfaite*, ascends by only one degree."

37. Saint Lambert never returns to this discussion of the imperfect cadence, although he points to three different types of imperfect cadences in exx. 58, 95, 99, 103-11--and he provides another in ex. 129.

It is clear from his examples that Saint Lambert's imperfect cadences do not conform to the modern use of the term--as applied to cadences whose final chord is not in root position, or whose highest part does not end on the tonic. This latter definition is given in Masson (*Nouveau traité des règles pour la composition*, pp. 50-55):

> La Cadence imparfaite, que d'autres appellent rompuë, est celle ou la Partie superieure ne se termine pas sur la même corde que la Basse; c'est-à-dire, qu'elle fait un autre accord avec la Basse au lieu de faire l'octave, soit dans le Mode majeur soit dans le Mode mineur.

> [The imperfect Cadence, which others call interrupted, is the one in which the upper Part does not end on the same pitch as the Bass; that is, it forms another interval [i.e., the Third or Fifth, as Masson's examples show] with the Bass instead of forming the Octave--either in the major Mode or in the minor Mode.]

Masson then explains (p. 51) that the bass can make a cadence imperfect either by descending a Third instead of a Fifth, or by ascending one degree instead of a Fourth, to its final note.

Saint Lambert's imperfect cadences conclude on a dominant or on a secondary dominant (in some of his examples, the underlying tonality is open to question), and his three categories appear to be distinguished by three different melodic approaches to the final bass note: (1) a descending, Phrygian approach (ex. 58, ex. 95 [C-D], exx. 107-09, ex., 129 [2nd cadence], (2) a descending, stepwise approach (ex. 95 [A-B], exx. 103-06, exx. 110-11, and (3) a cadence in which the final bass note is approached by the upward leap of a Fifth or the downward leap of a Fourth (ex. 99).

This third type of cadence conforms to Masson's *cadence irregulière* (*Nouveau traité des règles pour la composition*, pp. 54-55; see Ch. 7, n. 9). Masson continues by saying "One can call this Cadence imperfect if one wishes, because the upper Part does not end on the same pitch as the Bass."

According to the *Encyclopédie*, the common usage
of the term *cadence imparfaite* is applied to the
dominant cadence approached by an upward leap of a
Fifth.

38. Here and elsewhere in his treatise, Saint
Lambert's terminology refers to the older hexachord
system (*la Gamme* or *la Méthode des Muances*), which
was gradually being replaced at this time in France
by the fixed do system (*la Méthode du Si*). Loulié
(*Elements ou principes de musique*, pp. 48-49; trans.
Cohen, pp. 43-44) and Masson (*Nouveau traité des
règles pour la composition*, p. 12) present both
systems. Mattheson (*Große General-Baß-Schule*,
"Letztes Prob=Stück der Ober=Claße," 12, pp. 449-50)
ridicules the excess verbiage of Saint Lambert's an-
tiquated terminology; see Ch. 4, n. 13.

39. See pp. 97-99.

CHAPTER 4

1. The *Encyclopédie* lists the following meanings
for *ton*: (1) tonality, (2) instrumental or vocal
range, (3) pitch-pipe, and (4) the fundamental tonic
pitch of a piece.

2. Again, Saint Lambert's terminology derives
from the hexachord system, whereby a pitch of the
gamut is identified by its letter name together with
the syllables corresponding to its position in one
or more hexachords; see above, Ch. 3, n. 38.

3. "A subject in musical terms is what the principal melody is called, upon which the entire layout
[*disposition*] of a musical piece unfolds [*roule*], &
to which all the other parts but serve as accompaniment. Sometimes the subject is in the bass, but
more often in the upper parts and rarely in the
middle parts" (*Encyclopédie*, s.v. *Sujet*). Masson
(*Nouveau traité des règles pour la composition*, p.
13 and pp. 16-21) gives detailed directions for
composing a musical subject.

4. According to Loulié (*Elements ou principes de
musique*, p. 65), "The *Major Mode*, & the *Minor Mode*
each have three Notes that are called *Principal
Tones* or *Essential Tones* of the Mode.   The Note that

concludes each Piece of Music is called the Final;
the Third from this Final is called the *Mediant*; the
Fifth from this same Final is called the *Dominant*."

5. Saint Lambert's original statement [*qu'il
roule sur les cordes d'une modulation*] might best be
translated "that the Air proceeds by the essential
and natural pitches of the mode"--in accordance with
Brossard's definition of the term *modulation* (see
Preface, n. 11).

6. The parallel structure of this sentence and
the previous one shows that here Saint Lambert uses
the terms *modulation* and *mode* synonymously.

7. In the hexachord system, B-natural is referred
to as *B mi* by virtue of its position as the third
pitch in the hard hexachord on G (*hexachordum du-
rum*), and B-flat is called *B fa* because it is the
fourth pitch in the soft hexachord on F (*hexachordum
molle*). While (in hexachordal terminology) Saint
Lambert's addition of *Bemol* to the term *B Fa Si
Bemol* (*B Fa Si-Flat*) is redundant, his term *B Fa Si
Becarre* (*B Fa Si-Natural*) is contradictory.

8. The use of the older terminology *Becarre* and
Bemol to indicate major and minor is also used in
Delair's *Traité d'acompagnement* and in Masson's
Nouveau traité des règles pour la composition.

9. Johann Mattheson translates this passage in
Große General-Baß-Schule, "Vorbereitung zur Or-
ganisten=Probe," CCXIV (Hamburg: Johann Kißner,
1731), pp. 126-27:

> Wir brauchen anitzo wircklich / alle Stunde und
> Augenblick / in jeder Octave / fast in jedem Liede
> / unumgänglich elff / wo nicht zwölff Klänge / und
> sollen doch nur sieben davon zu Rathe ziehen; un-
> geachtet der eine Klang eben so viel gilt / als
> der andre / und hier weder Rang / noch Natur den
> geringsten Vorzug gibt. Das wäre zwar auf gewis-
> se Art eine Octave / aber nichts weniger / als ein
> Diapason / davon St. Lambert sagt / *es gehören
> wenigstens zwölff Theile dazu / welche zwölff ver-
> schiedene Klänge geben / deren jeder zum Grund=Ton
> eines Gesanges geleget werden kann / und daher wir
> zwölff Ton=Arten in unsrer Music behaupten mögen.*
> Diese zwölff werden hiernechst / durch Veränderung

der Tertziens also verdoppelt / daß vier und
zwantzig tonische Moden daraus entstehen.

10. That is, C#/D♭, D#/E♭, E#/F, F#/G♭, G#/A♭,
A#/B♭, B/C♭, B#/C.

11. Saint Lambert here gives the most complete
listing of tonalities (including enharmonic equi-
valents) up to this time. Jean Rousseau (*Méthode
claire, certain et facile pour aprendre à chanter la
musique* [Amsterdam: Roger, 1678]) was the first
French theorist to specifically discuss major and
minor modes, but he lists only thirteen tonalities;
Masson (*Nouveau traité des règles de la composition*)
lists sixteen tonalities.

12. Saint Lambert's labelling of the "rare" tonalities is not entirely consistent with his statement in *Les Principes du clavecin* (p. 38):

> Pour commencer par la Transposition par Diéze,
> nous dirons Qu'il y a sept degrez de Transposi-
> tion; c'est-à-dire, que les clefs peuvent être
> accompagnées d'un, de deux, de trois Diézes, jus-
> qu'au nombre de sept: mais il est rare qu'elles
> soient accompagnées de plus de trois.

> [Beginning with Transposition by Sharp, we will
> say that there are seven degrees of Transposition;
> that is, that the clefs may be accompanied by one,
> two, or by three Sharps--up to seven in number:
> but it is rare that they might be accompanied by
> more than three.]

But in his listing of the tonalities here, Saint
Lambert labels F-sharp minor as "rare"--but not E
major. In speaking of flat tonalities in *Les Principes* (p. 39), Saint Lambert states:

> La Transposition par Bémol a comme celle dont
> nous venons de parler sept degrez differens; c'est
> -à-dire que les clefs peuvent être accompagnées de
> Bémols jusqu'au nombre de sept, mais pour l'ordi-
> naire elles n'en ont pas plus de deux.

> [Transposition by Flats has, as does the one
> that we just discussed, seven different degrees;
> that is, that the clefs may be accompanied by up
> to seven Flats, but ordinarily they have not more
> than two.]

But in his listing here, Saint Lambert labels A-flat major as "rare"--but not C minor, F minor, or E-flat major.

13. Mattheson quotes this passage in *Große General-Baß-Schule*, "Letztes Prob=Stück der Ober=Claße," 12, pp. 449-50:

> Es stehet wol zu vermuthen / daß nach etlichen hundert Jahren / falls diese Welt noch so lange im Stande bleibet / die Componisten und Virtuosen das **Cis dur** / **B moll** &c eben so leicht abfertigen werden / als unsere Dorff=Organisten ihr **C dur** / welches schier aus der Mode zu seyn scheinet / und heutiges Tages eben so selten / als vormahls häuffig / angetroffen wird. Es ist auch mit den Tonen einiger massen eben so bewandt / als mit andern Dingen / und was vor hundert Jahren eine Ehre war / dessen schämet man sich auf gewisse Art bey itzigen Zeiten. St. Lambert redet davon also: "Unter den Tonen sind etliche, die man mehr gebraucht / als andere. Es sind deren so gar einige / die vielleicht doch nie zum Grunde einer Melodie gedienet haben; aber ich habe sie darum doch nicht ausschliessen wollen / indem die meisten Componisten schon verschiedene davon gebrauchen / welche vorhin nicht berühret wurden / und weil es wol kommen könnte / daß man sie endlich alle mit einander gleich gemein machte."

But he disagrees with Saint Lambert's inclusion of two tonalities among those that are rarely used. Regarding B Major:

> Dieser Ton / **H dur** / heisset / nach des Herrn von St. Lamberts rothwelschen Mund=Art: *B Fa Si Becare majeure*, und stehet abermahl (ich weiß in aller Welt nicht warum?) dabey geschrieben: *rare*. Wenn wir lauter Raritäten aus unsern Tonen machen wollen / so wundert mich nicht / daß die Armuth der General=Bassisten so groß ist. Stünde gleich in der Fibel / bey dem Q / X / Y / u.s.w / daß es rare Buchstaben wären / weil sie nicht so offt / als A / E / I / O / U / vorkommen; so könnte doch solches den Lesebengel nicht entschuldigen / wenn er sie nicht kennte / noch vielweniger einen Buch-

drucker / wenn sie in seiner Werckstatt nicht ge-
funden werden sollten.

and F# Minor:

Msr. St. Lambert nennet diesen Ton p. 29. *F ut Fa
Dièze mineur,* und schreibet dabey: *Rare.* **Fis mol**
ist kürtzer gesagt / und bey mir nichts rares.

14. Mattheson (*ibid.*, 21, p. 456) here critici-
zes Saint Lambert's awkward method of notating
double accidentals:

Ob aber diese Verdoppelung der # und *b* nicht mehr
Verwirrung machet / als wenn / obberührter massen
/ die zierlichern Säiten mit einem *x* / oder * /
oder dreifachen Kreutz / in dem Lauff der Melodie
/ bezeichnet würden / lasse jedem zum Urtheil
über.

15. In his examples Saint Lambert is inconsistent
with his manner of cancelling sharps and flats: he
cancels a flat with a natural sign in the music
(e.g., ex. 55), while in his figures he cancels a
flat with a sharp (e.g., ex. 48, 49, and 55). These
kinds of notational inconsistencies are symptomatic
of French music of this period in general. Delair
(*Traité d'acompagnement*) suggests using a natural to
cancel a flat; later, Michel Pignolet de Montéclair
(*Nouvelle méthode pour aprendre la musique* [Paris:
Chez l'auteur, 1709]) recommends the natural to
cancel a sharp. Bernier (*Principes de composition*)
uses a flat in the music to cancel a sharp in the
key signature, and a sharp in the music to cancel a
flat in the key signature; to cancel sharps or flats
in the music, Bernier uses the natural sign.

In his earlier treatise (*Les Principes du Clavecin*, p. 37 and pp. 62-64), Saint Lambert allowed a
flat in the music to be cancelled by either a sharp
or a natural, while he permits a sharp to be cancelled only by a flat.

Saint Lambert also does not follow the rules he
set forth in *Les Principes du Clavecin* governing how
accidentals apply to repeated notes of the same
degree. He stated in the earlier treatise (pp. 35-
36) that the notated accidental controls all consecutive repetitions of the same pitch (irrespective

of intervening barlines), and is cancelled only by a change in pitch; here in several examples, however, he notates redundant accidentals (e.g. ex. 69).

16. See p. 63, rule 5, and pp. 78-80, rules 1-4 for further discussion of the raised bass note.

17. Here Saint Lambert seems to return to his original use of the term *modulation*--designating the essential and natural pitches of the mode from which derive the melody and harmony; see Preface, n. 11.

CHAPTER 5

1. For exceptions to this rule, see pp. 105-106, Rules 10-13. Marc-Antoine Charpentier's treatise *Règles de composition* (repr. Lillian M. Ruff, "Marc-Antoine Charpentier's *Règles de composition*," *The Consort*, XXIV [1967], 233-70) forbids consecutive perfect Fifths, but permits consecutive Octaves:

> La quinte seule determine l'accord; c'est pourquoy il n'en faut jamais faire deux de suitte a moins qu'ils ne soient de differente espece pour ne pas blesser la diversite qui fait toutte l'essence de la musique. . . plusieurs Octaves de suitte entre les Parties et meme contre la Basse ne font point de faute par ce qu'elles ne determinent point les accords.

> [The fifth alone determines the chord; this is why one must never play two in succession unless they are of different species, so as not to mar the diversity which is the very essence of music. . . several consecutive Octaves between the Parts (and even against the Bass) are not a mistake, because they do not determine the chords.]

2. This would be e' or f', as shown on the "Démonstration du Clavier" printed in Saint Lambert's *Les Principes du clavecin*, p. 6 (repr. in Harris-Warrick, p. 18). The reason for this rule is explained by Heinichen (*Der General-Baß in der Composition*, p. 548, n. h; translated in George J. Buelow, *Thorough-Bass Accompaniment according to Johann*

David Heinichen [University of California Press, 1966], p. 68): "When the old theorists gave the rule that one should not readily go higher than c" with the right hand or, on any account, not above e", they sought in this way to prevent too great a vacuum or empty space between both hands in the accompaniments of their time, which were both very thin and usually in three parts." The one exception that permits the right hand to move higher on the keyboard, according to Saint Lambert, is "when the Bass becomes Alto"--that is, when the bass part, played by the left hand, ascends into the range generally reserved for the right hand.

3. In roughly half of his examples containing a Seventh, Saint Lambert breaks the rule that requires the Seventh to resolve downwards; ascending Sevenths can be found (usually in the context of perfect cadences) in: exx. 23, 34-38, 40, 44, 55, 90, 98, and 116-22.

4. Notice how Saint Lambert, in exx. 47 and 48 (and later in exx. 57 and 69), takes the final chord in five parts to ensure the descending resolution of the Seventh.

CHAPTER 6

1. The three orders of the perfect chord were discussed on pp. 20-21, and are distinguished by the Third, Fifth, or Octave being the highest part.

2. See p. 101-102, Rule 4.

3. See pp. 100-101, Rules 1-3.

4. An uninflected note (*une note naturelle*) differs from a Natural note (*un Becarre*) in that *une note naturelle* is the pitch determined by the key and the mode, while *un Becarre* would be a chromatic alteration of a *note naturelle* in a transposed key. Chromatic motion in the bass is further discussed on pp. 78-80, Rules 1-4.

5. Saint Lambert mentioned this previously on pp. 34-35.

6. Here Saint Lambert provides a different definition of the slur (*liaison*) than that which he introduced in *Les Principes du clavecin*, pp. 12-14

(trans. in Harris-Warrick, pp. 29-31). In his earlier treatise, Saint Lambert explains that all of
the slurred notes are played, held, and released at
once with the last note contained within a slur (he
then cites a number of exceptions to this general
rule). The examples cited above (exx. 23, 35, 47,
52) evidently do not follow this rule.

7. Saint Lambert does not follow this rule in ex.
11 (mm. 1, 3, and 5) and in exx. 107-08.

8. In other words, chords adjacent to a chromati-
cally inflected bass note must adopt that inflection
--presumably to avoid a cross relation. Regarding
the distinction between *naturel* and *becarre*, see Ch.
6, n. 4 above.

9. This imperfect cadence might be described as a
bass that descends stepwise a Fourth (from a to e)
with a semitone falling between the penultimate and
final note (i.e., a Phrygian descent) and with the
penultimate note bearing two chords. The first bass
note bears a minor perfect chord which is retained
on the second bass note; the third bass note bears a
Seventh chord, followed by a little chord (i.e., a
$^6_4$) and the last bears a perfect dominant chord (with
^{3}
a raised Third; c.f., ex. 95 [C-D].

On pp. 113-14, Saint Lambert recommends playing a
trill on the penultimate bass note of an imperfect
cadence (one that concludes by stepwise motion), as
can be seen above in ex. 58.

10. See p. 13.

11. That is, F-G#, Bb-C#, and Eb-F#; Saint Lambert neglects to include the augmented seconds C-D#,
Db-E, Gb-A, and Ab-B.

12. The full implication of Saint Lambert's
statement may not be immediately apparent to the
modern reader. In *Les Principes du clavecin*, p. 64,
Saint Lambert explains that:

> One usually calls transposed Pieces those in which
> the Clefs are accompanied by Sharps or Flats
> [i.e., those that have key signatures]; but it is
> wrong to call them this without any further dis-
> tinction--for there are several [pieces] that,
> having many Flats or Sharps, are not transposed at
> all, & are on the contrary in very natural modes.
> Such are Pieces in D La Ré Béquarre [D-major], in

A Mi La Béquarre [A-major], in B Fa Si Bémol
tierce majeure [Bb-major], & several others. The
only truly transposed modes are those in which the
Chords are not in their usual pure state, as in
several in which the major Thirds are more than
major, & others in which the minor [Thirds] are
less than minor—in a word, those in which the intervals are either too large or too small. If I
thus called all of them transposed, it was solely
to conform to the usual custom—combined with [the
fact] that the trueness or the falsity of transposition of these types of Pieces does not affect
the rule in question in Chapter XVIII.

By "transposed tonalities" (*tons transposez*), Saint
Lambert evidently means tonalities in which the in-
tonation is so distorted that minor Thirds become
equivalent to augmented Seconds. This phenomenon is
normative in equal temperament, where the division
of the Octave into equal semitones results in augmented Seconds and minor Thirds which sound alike
out of context. But in Saint Lambert's day, mean-
tone tuning was far more prevalent; here, the pure
tuning of Thirds results in semitones of different
sizes (see the *Encyclopédie*, s.v. *Tempérament*).
With respect to the keyboard depicted in *Les Principes du clavecin* (p. 6; repr. in Harris-Warrick, p.
18) where accidentals are tuned to C#, Eb, F#, G#,
and Bb, the minor Third above F, for example, would
be G#—which would be lower in pitch than Ab in the
mean-tone system, and hence would be one of those
minor Thirds that Saint Lambert calls "less than
minor."

13. Delair (*Traité d'acompagnement*, p. 25) gives
a more complete listing of the *falsae* and mentions
that the augmented Second is favored particularly by
Italian composers.

14. Ex. 34 on p. 38 illustrates this rule, where-
by the second Bass note bears the figure $\overset{9}{7}$ and retains the perfect chord of the previous bass note.

15. Saint Lambert presumably prescribes this rule
in order to avoid parallel Octaves in the right
hand; Boyvin (*Traité abrégé de l'accompagnement*, p.
77) also forbids consecutive perfect chords, doubled
Sixth chords, or simple chords.

CHAPTER 7

1. According to Saint Lambert's first rule (p. 78), in the following example the second chord of m. 2 and of m. 5 should be figured with a 6 and accompanied with a doubled chord $^6_6$ or $^6_3$; an earlier rule (pp. 26-27) stated that the false Fifth is combined with the Third and the Sixth, rather than with the Third and the Octave as shown in mm. 1, 2, 4, and 5 of ex. 83.

2. In other words, rules 8, 9, and 10 state that the Third of a chord should be minor or major, depending on whether the pitch that forms the minor or major Third appeared in the bass one or two notes before or after that chord. Rule 12 is a similar rule for the diminished Fifth.

3. In exx. 38, 77, 94, and 123, Saint Lambert uses the doubled chord ($^6_3$ or $^3_6$) on the second bass note instead of the simple chord of the Sixth $^8_6$; in ex. 85 and 123 he uses the perfect chord on the $^3_3$ second bass note.

4. In the original French, "double" is misspelled "bouble," and "6" is missing from the figure $^6_5$.

5. Cf. p. 64, Rule 8.

6. The first of these examples (A-B) shows a bass line that descends stepwise a Fourth (from g to d) with a semitone between the second and third notes and with the penultimate note repeated and bearing two chords. The first bass note bears a perfect major chord which is retained on the second bass note; the third bass note bears a Seventh chord and then the simple chord of the major Sixth $^8_6$; the last ^{3} chord bears a perfect minor chord.

The second example (C-D) is similar to ex. 58 in that the semitone falls between the penultimate and final bass note (as before, a Phrygian approach to the cadence); here, however, the penultimate chord is the chord of the doubled Third, which cadences on a dominant chord. On pp. 112-13, Rule 15, Saint Lambert recommends playing a trill on the penultimate bass note of an imperfect cadence that concludes by stepwise motion, as seen in letters C-D of the above example.

7. Saint Lambert's exx. 3, 9, 42, and 85 do not follow this rule.

8. According to the first rule of this chapter (p. 78), the second bass note of m. 1 and m. 3 of ex. 97 would require the doubled chord $\frac{6}{3}$ or $\frac{6}{3}$; Saint Lambert does not follow this rule in exx. 22, 25, 48, 83, and 126.

9. Ex. 99 contains four imperfect cadences (which Saint Lambert says are of the same type) in which the bass rises by semitone and then ascends a Fifth (the first two cadences) or descends a Fourth (the last two cadences). The first bass note bears a $\frac{6}{5}$ chord; the second bass note bears either a perfect chord (cadences 1 and 3) or a simple chord of the major Sixth $\frac{8}{6}{}_3$ (cadences 2 and 4); and the last bass note bears a dominant chord.

This type of cadence is similar to the irregular cadence (or the "half cadence," in modern terminology) described by Masson (*Nouveau traité des règles de la composition*, p. 54):

> Il y a encore une sorte de Cadence aussi bien dans le Mode majeur que dans le Mode mineur, qu'on peut appeler irreguliére, qui se fait à la dominante, & qui est toute opposée à celle que la Basse fait par degrez disjoints, parce qu'elle tombe à la dominante d'une quarte seulement, & y monte d'une quinte.

> [There is furthermore one type of Cadence found in the major as well as in the minor mode that could be called irregular; this Cadence is formed on the dominant, & is the exact opposite of the one that the Bass forms by disjunct degrees-- because it falls to the dominant solely by a Fourth & rises to it by a Fifth.]

10. Saint Lambert did not strictly follow this rule in exx. 56 and 57, where he shows the chord on the third bass note played with contrary motion.

11. Saint Lambert does not follow this rule in exx. 21 and 128. Regarding the consecutive Fifths between the upper two parts in the following example, see p. 105, rule 10.

12. In *Les Principes du clavecin*, pp. 43-47 and pp. 64-65 (trans. in Harris-Warrick, pp. 76-82),

Saint Lambert discusses the trill *(tremblement)* in detail. Briefly, he states that (1) the trill begins with the upper neighbor [his examples show it struck on the beat, simultaneously with other notated parts], (2) the upper neighbor adopts any accidental immediately or closely preceding it, (3) the trill is played either by the first [thumb] and second finger or by the second and third finger of the left hand, (4) the duration of the note determines the duration of the trill, (5) on a long note, the trill could be played slowly at first, and accelerate toward the end, (6) on a short note, the trill must be quick, (7) the trill should end with the main note. Ex. 102, therefore, should have two short trills beginning on c' and f respectively, played by fingers 1 and 2; ex. 107-09 should have short trills beginning on c, played by fingers 2 and 3; and ex. 129 should have short trills beginning on e and c respectively, played by fingers 2 and 3 (or, for the trill on d, possibly by fingers 1 and 2). For more on the trill, see pp. 112-13, rule 15.

13. Exx. 103 and 104 show an imperfect cadence in which the bass line descends stepwise a Fourth, with the semitone falling between the first and second bass notes; in exx. 105 and 106, the semitone falls between the second and third bass notes (as in ex. 95, A-B).

Exx. 107-09 are similar to exx. 58 and 95 in that the semitone in the stepwise descent of a Fourth falls between the penultimate and final bass note (a Phrygian cadence); as in these two other examples, Saint Lambert notates a trill on the penultimate bass note.

14. These cadences are of the stepwise, non-Phrygian variety described in Ch. 3, n. 37 and in Ch. 7, n. 13; see also ex. 95 (A-B), exx. 103-06.

15. In other words, one would accompany passages that do not end on the downbeat of the measure the same way as shown in the examples of Rule 24 and 25 (exx. 103-11).

16. The cadence was previously introduced in Chapter 3, Article 6, pp. 44-46.

17. See p. 105, rule 9.

CHAPTER 8

1. See p. 74, rule 21.

2. The *basses de violons* played the *basse* part (the lowest part) in the typical five-part French orchestra of this time (with the *dessus* [the upper part] played by violins, and the *haute-contre*, *taille*, and *quinte* [the inner string parts] played by various sizes of violas). For further information see Jurgen Eppelsheim, *Das Orchester in den Werken Jean-Baptiste Lullys* (Tutzing: Hans Schneider, 1961).

3. Heinichen (*Der General-Baß in der Composition*, p. 565, n. k; trans. Buelow, *Thorough-Bass Accompaniment*, p. 179) also condones adding passagework in the bass at the accompanist's discretion. Heinichen's directions echo the words of Saint Lambert:

> Not all composers are content with these bass variations. Nevertheless if, for example, in a solo, a cantata *a voce sola*, or in the empty ritornello of an aria without instruments, such things are introduced *à propos* and with discernment, they embellish the accompaniment and are certainly admissible. Only one must not irritate the singer with these things and [must] not make a prelude out of the accompaniment.

4. According to the *Encyclopédie*, the term *concert* refers to either: (1) an assemblage of voices and instruments usually numbering at least four or five musicians, (2) the music itself, either vocal or instrumental, but in several parts, or (3) a musical organization maintained by private individuals, such as the *Concert of Marseille*, or *Toulouse*, or of *Bourdeaux*. The term *concertant* or *parties concertantes* can refer to a soloist or soloists in a large ensemble, or it can be used more generally to speak of the number of musicians in an ensemble--as with "a *concert* of eight to ten *concertans*."

5. Mattheson, *Große General-Baß-Schule*, "Letztes Prob=Stück," 31, p. 463 quotes this rule in its entirety.

6. This is the opposite of rule 6 above, where Saint Lambert recommends shifting the bass an Octave lower to avoid encumbering the hands. Heinichen (*Der General-Baß in der Composition*, p. 199; trans. Buelow, *Thorough-Bass Accompaniment*, p. 67) gives similar directions in order to free up the hands:

> [With the] numerous descending resolutions of dissonances, the right hand often comes down so low [on the keyboard] that it has no room left for resolutions, nor can the left hand (even if it takes the bass in the lowest octave) act freely. Therefore, a beginner...need only observe the two following suggestions with which he can again bring the right hand higher [on the keyboard], for example:
>
> (1) After the resolution of the dissonance occurs, or even on bass notes with no dissonances above them (particularly long notes), he seeks to halve the value and to break the chord so that the right hand, bit by bit, regains a higher position and wins a new place from which to bring about the resolution of the following dissonances.
>
> (2) He can, now and then, take a full-voiced chord high up [on the keyboard], and on the following bass note can again omit the lower part...

7. According to the *Encyclopédie*, a *choeur* is "a piece in full harmony in four or more parts sung by all the voices and played by the entire orchestra.

8. Saint Lambert's permissive attitude toward parallel Fifths and Octaves is not much different than many of his French contemporaries. While Nivers absolutely forbids parallels, Boyvin permits more license in accompaniment than in composition. Delair permits Fifths formed in contrary motion as well as consecutive Fifths of different types. See also n. 9 below.

Perhaps inadvertently, Saint Lambert gives an example of parallel Fifths between the upper parts of ex. 102.

9. Charpentier (Ruff, "Marc-Antoine Charpentier's *Règles de composition*," 259) permits composed passages of parallel Fifths in the upper parts, provided that the first or last Fifth is either augmented or diminished.

10. Heinichen (*Der General-Baß in der Composi-tion*, p. 132n) is not as quick to excuse hidden parallel Fifths and Octaves; he quotes Saint Lambert's last sentence above (*ibid.*, 133n)--but issues a further warning "that they [hidden parallel Fifths and Octaves] must be so surrounded by their adjacent parts or by so many inner parts that is it difficult or impossible to distinguish them:"

Weil sie von denen aussersten Stimmen verdecket, und also mit *raison*, durch die gewöhnliche Verwechselung der Stimmen entschuldiget werden; wie es denn hier nach *Lamberts* Ausspruch, in oben gedachten seinem *Traetat* vom General-Bass heisset: *Comme la Musique n'est faite que pour l'oreille, une faute, qui ne l'offense pas, n'est pas une faute:* Die *Music* ist allein vor die Ohren gemacht, also ist derienige Fehler vor keinen Fehler zu rechnen, welcher die Ohren nicht beleidiget. Mann muß aber auch acht haben, daß dergleichen Fehler die Ohren in der That nicht beleidigen, *i.e.* daß sie von ihren nechsten Stimmen so umgeben, oder von der Menge der Mittel=Stimmen so überschüttet werden, daß sie das Gehöre schwerlich oder gar nicht unterscheiden möge: sonst seynd sie allerdings, (ich meyne, wenn sie fein treuhertzig in der Menge begangen werden,) unter eben diejenigen *Grammaticalischen* Fehler zu rechnen, welche nicht einmahl die Entschuldigung eines: *errare humanum,* oder menschlichen Versehens leiden.

CHAPTER 9

1. Some of Saint Lambert's ideas on good taste are anticipated in Delair's *Traité d'acompagnement,* p. 5:

Toute sortes d'Instruments ne sont pas propres pour accompagner, dautant qu'il ne faut pas dans l'accompagnement que les dessus dominent sur les basses, par ce qu'il n'est pas question de faire briller l'instrument lors que l'on accompagne, mais seulement de soutenir la voix qu'on accompagne. Ainsi il faut que les basses y dominent,

c'est la raison pour laquelle on ne se sert pas
ordinairement du Luth, ni de la Guitarre pour accompagner, dautant que les dessus y dominent trop,
et les basses ni fournissent pas assez.

[All types of Instruments are not equally suitable for accompanying, insofar as in the accompaniment the treble should not dominate over the
bass; because it is not a matter of showing off
the instrument [i.e., playing soloistically] when
one accompanies, but rather to use it to support
the voice one accompanies. Thus the bass [regis-
ter] must dominate there, and this is the reason
why one does not usually employ the Lute or the
Guitar to accompany--insofar as the treble
[strings] dominate too much, and the bass
[strings] do not provide enough support.]

2. Again, Saint Lambert's advice is anticipated
in Delair's *Traité d'acompagnement*, pp. 22-23:

Le premier accord est l'accord naturel, lequel
consiste en la tierce, la quinte, et l'octaue; on
se peut neantmoins passer de l'octaue, la tierce
et la quinte étant un acompagnement sufisant,
principalement sur le theorbe, ou l'on ne trouue
pas facilement tous les accords sous la main, sur
tout dans les pieces transposées et de mouuement
leger.

[The first chord is the natural chord, which
consists of the Third, Fifth, and Octave; nevertheless, one can leave out the Octave since the
Third and Fifth are a sufficient accompaniment--
particularly on the theorbo, where one does not
easily find all of the chords at hand, especially
in transposed pieces and those in quick tempo.]

3. In other words, for dissonant chords, one may
double only the Second and fill in with consonant
chord tones (because in this case the Second repre-
sents the real root of the chord, and the bass note
is the transposed Seventh). And for Seventh chords,
one may fill in with the Third, the Fifth, and the
Octave. Presumably the suspended Seventh would not
be accompanied or doubled in this way, since the

Sixth, not the Octave, is the consonance replacing the Seventh.

Saint Lambert's filled-in accompaniment is conservative compared to that discussed by two earlier French authors. D'Anglebert's *Pieces de clavecin* (pp. 123-28) is the earliest source in France to discuss the full-voiced style. Here, d'Anglebert advises filling in the left hand primarily with consonances, but he also allows some dissonance doublings (Seconds and Tritones). Kenneth Gilbert, in the preface to his edition of d'Anglebert's *Pièces de clavecin* (Paris: Heugel, 1975; p. vii), states:

> The importance of the short treatise on figured-bass playing should not be underestimated. Apart from the composer's statement that it contains all one needs to know about the subject in order to perfect oneself--surely a clue to the character of the accompaniment in his time--the examples are notable for their low-lying texture, and for regular use of filled-in chords in the right hand together with octave doublings in the left. This is far more likely to represent actual keyboard practice of the time than the scholastic four-part examples in Saint-Lambert's treatise (1707).

Delair's *Traité d'acompagnement* of the following year also discusses filled-in accompaniment (pp. 57-58):

> La pluspart des acords qui se font de la main gauche, ne sont que pour remplir le wide qui se rencontre entre les deux mains d'autant que l'on doit faire ordinairement les acords les plus essentiels de la main droite.
>
> Quand il y a quelque dissonnance, marquée sur la basse, on la doit ordinairement faire de la main droite, auec ses acompagnemens les plus essentiels faisant les autres acompagnemens de la main gauche, ou doublant de ladite main gauche, ceux que l'on fait de la droite.
>
> [Most of the chords played by the left hand serve only to fill in the gap that occurs between the two hands--more especially as one should usu-

ally play the most essential chords with the right
hand.

When there is a dissonance marked above the
bass, one should usually play it with the right
hand with its most essential accompaniments--while
either playing with the left hand the other accompaniments, or doubling with the left hand those
(accompaniments) that one plays in the right.]

Regarding dissonance-doubling, Delair in his Preface
[xi-xii] advocates filling in with the Second and
Tritone:

> On peut doubler de la main gauche, toutes les
> consonances qui convienent aux accords que l'on
> acompagne, on peut meme doubler tous les acompag-
> nements de la seconde, aussi bien que la seconde
> même, on peut aussi doubler les acompagnemens du
> triton, et le triton même, on ne double point la
> fausse quinte, la septieme, ni la neufvieme.

> [One may double with the left hand all of the
> consonances that pertain to the chords one plays
> as accompaniment; one may even double all of the
> accompaniments of the Second, as well as the Sec-
> ond itself; one may also double the accompaniments
> of the Tritone, and the Tritone itself; one does
> not double the false Fifth, the Seventh, or the
> Ninth.]

Heinichen (*Der General-Baß in der Composition*) provides a detailed description of full-voiced accompaniment supported by numerous examples, and he allows
the doubling of any dissonance in the left hand. A
summary of Heinichen's instructions appears in Buelow, *Thorough-Bass Accompaniment*, pp. 72-89.

4. This procedure would result in a $^6_5$ chord;
Saint Lambert's directions allowing the Fifth (the
dissonance in this chord) to be doubled stand in
conflict with Rule 4 above.

5. In *Les Principes du clavecin*, pp. 54-56
(trans. Harris-Warrick, pp. 94-96), Saint Lambert
describes two kinds of arpeggios--the simple arpeggio (performed by separating the notes of a chord),
and the figured arpeggio (which includes neighboring
passing tones). His directions may be summed up as
follows: (1) the simple arpeggio is played on chords

of 2 to 4 notes, while the figured arpeggio is played only on chords of 3 to 4 notes; (2) simple arpeggios can be played from the bottom up or from the
top down, while figured arpeggios are nearly always
played from the bottom up; (3) with the exception of
the 2-note simple arpeggio, there should be no perceptible break between the arpeggiated notes; (4) in
figured arpeggios, borrowed notes are released and
the chord tones are held for full value; (5) three-
note chords may have one or two borrowed notes,
while four-note chords may have only one; (6) the
chord-fingerings that Saint Lambert recommends for
small hands (p. 41; trans. p. 71) are the appropriate ones for figured arpeggios.

    6. Heinichen (*Der General-Baß in der Composi-
tion*, p. 557) expands upon Saint Lambert's discussion of arpeggiated accompaniment (Buelow, *Thorough-
Bass Accompaniment*, p. 176):

> The *arpeggio* overshadows in importance all
> other embellishments of this second group. In its
> most common form a full-voiced chord is broken
> from the lowest note of the left hand to the high-
> est of the right. These arpeggios can also be
> played doubly (from the lowest to the highest tone
> and back to the lowest in reverse order) or repea-
> tedly (by repeating the double arpeggio one or
> more times). This last variety may conclude by
> striking a solid chord in the right hand "as is
> frequently applied to the harpsichord in the re-
> citative and with other motionless bass notes.
> Moreover, with somewhat active or moderately quick
> notes the left hand frequently plays a full-voiced
> chord with a simple arpeggio while the right hand
> concludes with a solid chord on the same beat.
> One must seek to learn from fine performers the
> many other similar ways of breaking [chords].

Heinichen also illustrates a wide variety of
chordal figurations which can be introduced into the
thoroughbass accompaniment; see Buelow, *Thorough-
Bass Accompaniment*, pp. 176-85.

    7. The concepts behind the terms *mesure* and *mou-
vement* have changed since Saint Lambert's time.
Mesure encompasses at once the modern concepts of
measure (as in a measure of music), meter, and mea-

sured proportion. The *Encyclopédie* defines *mesure*
as a way of dividing the duration or the beat into
several equal parts--each one of which is also called a *mesure*, and can also be divided into other
parts; the *Encyclopédie* then discusses different
types of *mesure* and the metric symbols associated
with them. *Mouvement*, according to the *Encyclopédie*, is "the degree of swiftness or slowness given
to the *mesure* in accordance with the character of
the air." In the context of the above paragraph,
les Airs de mouvement refers to pieces of predefined
character in a particular meter and tempo (e.g.,
dance airs).

Mouvement* also refers to the movement of the
hands made while conducting, which is articulated by
means of beats (*temps*). In *Les Principes du clavecin* (p. 20) Saint Lambert gives a vivid account of
how one conducts different types of *mesure*, and he
urges the performer to envisage these vigorous hand
motions even when playing solo:

> But since it is not possible to beat the Measure
> with the hand while playing the harpsichord, one
> must fill his head with the image of these move-
> ments--so as to beat it mentally and to regulate
> (according to this Measure being beaten in his
> head) the [rhythmic] Cadence of the pieces he
> plays.

8. Here it is evident that Saint Lambert has in
mind unmeasured music (as suggested by his use of
the term *Recitatif*) for Rule 9, as well as for Rules
10 and 11. At this time the term *récit* held the
more general meaning of a sung solo; *récitatif*, on
the other hand, refers to:

> . . .a way of singing which derives as much from
> declamation as from singing, as if one speaks
> while singing or sings while speaking; hence more
> attention is given to expressing emotions than
> following a regular measure precisely. This does
> not prevent this kind of singing from being no-
> tated in a regular meter, but one is given liberty
> to alter the length of the measure and to make
> some measures longer or shorter than others. This
> is why the basso-continuo is usually placed in the

score directly below the recitative so that the
accompanist can follow the singer rather than the
conductor. (Brossard, *Dictionnaire de musique*,
s.v. Recitativo; trans. Gruber)

9. Masson (*Nouveau traité des règles pour la composition*) devotes his tenth chapter to fugal composition (pp. 103-20). Masson defines "fugue" as "a
Melody [Chant] that must be repeated or imitated by
one or more Parts," and identifies four types: (1)
imitation of a melody at the Unison or Octave [*parfaite ressemblance ou répétition du même Chant*], (2)
imitation at the Fourth or Fifth [*simple imitation
de Chant*], (3) imitation by mirror inversion [*Con-
tre-Fugue ou Fugue renversée*], and (4) double fugue
[*double Fugue*].

Mattheson (*Große General-Baß-Schule*, "Neuntes
Prob=Stück," 3, p. 351) cites Rule 12 in its entirety:

> Es gefällt mir sonderlich wol / daß der Herr von
> St. Lambert es auch so gar gut heisset / wenn man
> eine eintzige Stimme *accompagnirt*, und den Haupt=
> Satz oder die Fugen der Arie mit allen Parteyen
> auf seinem Clavier dabey nachahmet. Seine Worte
> lauten auf Teutsch also: *Wenn man zu einer eint-
> zigen Sing=Stimme den General=Baß spielet / und
> etwa eine muntere / lebhaffte Arie vorkömmt / da-
> rin viele Nachahmungen anzutreffen sind / so wie
> wir sie in den Italiänischen Sachen finden; als-
> denn kann man auf seinem Clavier den Haupt=Satz
> und die fugen der Arie wolnachahmen / auch die
> Stimmen / eine nach der andern / anbringen.* Aber
> es gehöret eine völlige Wissenschafft dazu / und
> es muß ein Meister vom ersten Rang seyn dem sol-
> ches gut von Stattengehen soll. Hierunter können
> unsre Prob=Stück / als Muster / dienen. Ich hätte
> gerne etliche mehr von diesem ersten Rang in der
> Welt / es sind ihrer gar zu wenig. Die vom letz-
> ten Rang spielen den Meister allenthalben.

Heinichen also discusses imitating in the right-hand
accompaniment melodic motives originating in the
bass (*Der General-Baß in der Composition*, pp. 578-
79; trans. Buelow, *Thorough-Bass Accompaniment*, p.
188):

Finally, the second class of embellishments concludes with imitation, which differs from said embellishments in that it does not depend like the
former on our own ideas but must be taken from the
notated composition itself. Therefore, imitation
in this context results if an accompanist seeks to
imitate a composer's melodic motive or invention
in places where the composer himself HAS NOT USED
IT. The accompanist has few opportunities left
for imitation, because (1) one must never hinder a
singer or instrumentalist with these melodic motives, and, on the other hand, (2) one can expect
that a composer will himself fill out those places
where the imitation he has initiated will fit.
Thus, clearly on a keyboard instrument this em-
bellishment is the very poorest in use. Because,
however, rare cases can occur in a composition
(particularly in cantatas and arias without instruments) where a little place remains in which
the skilled accompanist can repeat a melodic motive begun in the thoroughbass or a concerted part
several times more than the composer has done, the
following example, therefore may serve as an illustration. Regarding which is still to be noted:
that the right hand seeks willingly to accompany
the concerted part in thirds and sixths and at the
same time to form a concerted duet with that part.
This form of imitation is particularly suited to
vocal pieces and is also easier to accomplish,
because in chamber and theatrical music one can
observe the singer exactly from the voice-part
usually written above [the thoroughbass], varying
from him and again following him.

10. For Nivers's and d'Anglebert's brief descrip-
tions of organ accompaniment, see Ch. 3, n. 1.
Heinichen (*Der General-Baß in der Composition*, Part
1, Chapter 2 "Von denen ordentlichen Accorden, und
wie selbige denen Incipienten nutzbar beyzubringen,"
p. 132n) warns against left-hand doublings on the
organ, "because the constant rumble of so many low
notes is unpleasing to the ears, and not infrequent-
ly will it become tiresome to the vocal or instrumental ensembles":

Je vollstimmiger man auf denen *Clavecins* mit bey-
den Händen *accompagniret,* ie harmoniöser fället es
aus. Hingegen darff man sich freylich auf Or-
geln, (sonderlich bey schwacher *Music* und ausser
dem *Tutti,*) nicht zusehr in das allzuvollstimmige
Accompagnement der lincken Hand verlieben, weil
das beständige Gemurre so vieler tieffen *Tone* dem
Ohre unangenehm, und dem *concertirenden* Sänger
oder *Instrumentisten* nicht selten beschwerlich
fället. Das *Judicium* muß hierbey das beste thun.

11. The second cadence of the following example
is one of Saint Lambert's imperfect cadences (with a
stepwise, Phrygian approach--as in exx. 58, 95 [C-
D], and 107-09). See Ch. 7, notes 6 and 13, and
also exx. 95 and 107-09.

Heinichen also gives detailed instructions for
the performance of trills in the right and left
hands of the thoroughbass (trans. Buelow, *Thorough-
Bass Accompaniment,* pp. 158-59).